DAVID THOMPSON

A Life of Adventure and Discovery

ELLE ANDRA-WARNER

HERITAGE

VICTORIA · VANCOUVER · CALGARY

Heritage House Publishing Company Ltd.
heritagehouse.ca

Library and Archives Canada Cataloguing in Publication
Andra-Warner, 1946–
    David Thompson: a life of adventure and discovery / Elle Andra-Warner.

ISBN 978-1-926613-32-1

    1.Thompson, David, 1770–1857. 2. Explorers—Canada—Biography. 3. Cartographers—Canada—Biography. 4. Fur traders—Canada—Biography. I. Title.

FC3212.1.T46A62 2010   971.0309   C2009-906903-2

Originally published 2006 by Altitude Publishing Canada Ltd.

Series editor: Lesley Reynolds
Proofreader: Karla Decker

Cover: "11th Koy Ape Falls to the Pacific Ocean—By the Grade of God," by Joseph Cross. To see more Joseph Cross paintings of David Thompson, visit www.josephcrossart.com.
The lyrics of the song "Map of Dreams" are reprinted with permission from Rodney Brown (www.rodneybrown.ca). The song appears on *The Big Lonely*.

The interior of this book was produced using 100% post-consumer recycled paper, processed chlorine free and printed with vegetable-based inks.

Heritage House acknowledges the financial support for its publishing program from the Government of Canada through the Canada Book Fund (CBF), Canada Council for the Arts and the province of British Columbia through the British Columbia Arts Council and the Book Publishing Tax Credit.

15 14 13 12   2 3 4 5

Printed in Canada

Contents

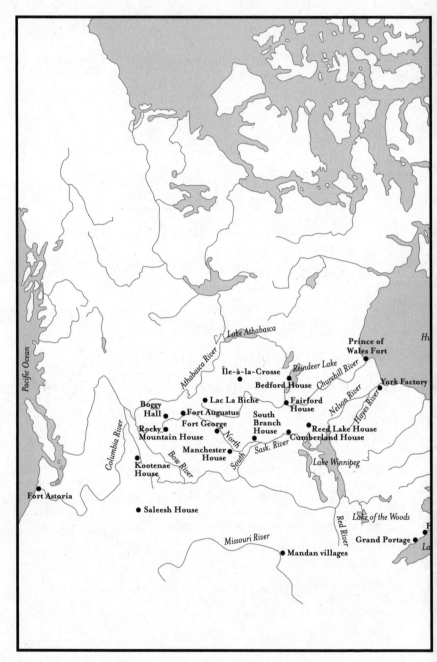

This map shows many of the fur-trade posts, lakes, rivers and other significant places associated with David Thompson.

ADAPTED FROM THE ATLAS OF CANADA WEBSITE, NATURAL RESOURCES CANADA.

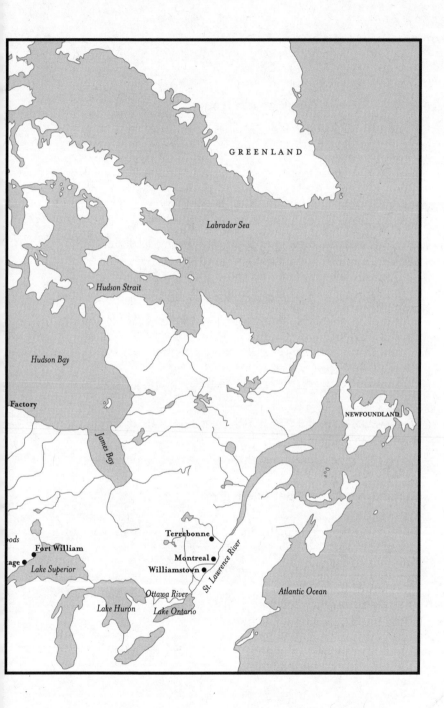

Map of Dreams

Rodney Brown

The mountains call me, now the rivers talk to me
I'm yearning for the western skies, I've a longing to be free
There's two ravens playing in flight, and I won't be alone
The stars may be my guide but this land is now my home.

Like Mackenzie and Fraser an explorer I'll be
I'll trace the shores, I'll draw the lines, I'll be the eyes of
    the company
No longer will I take my charge with the English Lords of
    the HBC
On the trail to the Canadians, it's a Nor'wester I'll be.

The new world in all its splendour, the rendezvous at
    Grand Portage
And oh the pipes they played that night, a thousand voices
    raised in song
The gifts they bring like an offering, my childhood dreams
    come true
The gift was men and north canoes, I'll draw my gift for you.

From Hudson Bay to Kitchi Onigaming
Up to Sault Ste. Marie
I'll draw the map of Canada
To the Western Sea

From the Pike Clan to the Assiniboine, the Peigans, the Bloods
    and the Cree
We learned the ways of the Blackfoot Nation, my Salish name
    was Koo Koo Sint
I was the man who looked at stars, the man who shared the
    pipe of peace
The man who listened and understood, the man you told
    your stories to.

From Hudson Bay to Kitchi Onigaming
Up to Sault Ste. Marie
I'll draw the map of Canada
To the Western Sea

Well, we found the Columbia at its source, we took the river
    to its end
We raised the Jack at Fort Astoria, and we laid claim to Oregon
The North West passage for the north canoes, for the voyageurs
    and the merchantmen
For Angus Bethune and the China trade, I drew the map for them.

The map was hung in Fort William at McGillivray's Great Hall
But the dreams of a western Canada no longer live inside its walls
Gone forever, the Nor'westers now, hope is lost the candle fades
The map of dreams will find a home—our dream will live again.

From Hudson Bay to Kitchi Onigaming
Up to Sault Ste. Marie
I drew the map of Canada
To the Western Sea.

To my grandson, Alexander Jack Brian Scott

Author's Note

Where necessary to ensure clarity, minor changes in spelling and punctuation have been made to quotations from David Thompson's writings.

Prologue

THE PLAN FOR THE 1801 *spring expedition of the North West Company was ambitious: cross the Rocky Mountains and reach the Pacific Ocean.*

On Sunday, June 7, 1801, the exploratory team, led by James Hughes with 31-year-old David Thompson as his second, rode out of Rocky Mountain House in a horseback brigade, not expecting to return until the following year. They followed the North Saskatchewan River and reached the Ram River three days later.

Four days into the trek, the brigade had already battled heavy rains, steep climbs, rough terrain, thunderstorms, floods, fast currents, deadfall and small bogs where some horses sank to their bellies. On June 11, as the pack horses edged their way along a steep, icy riverbank, one of them slipped and rolled down into the river, almost drowning. A short while later, another lost its footing, careened down a high hill and was stunned. Luckily, it recovered and continued on. A day later, the brigade walked on small and sharp pieces of broken rock that ripped through their shoes and lamed the horses.

On Saturday, June 13, they struggled through several feet of snow before reaching an impassable spot—a deep lake a mile long and a quarter-mile wide, surrounded by high cliffs. A small group, including Hughes and Thompson, went exploring on foot and at one point risked their lives by crawling on their hands and knees along a steep bank, a situation so dangerous that, according to Thompson, "the least slip would have precipitated us into the lake from a height of 100 feet."

Unable to find an alternative route for the horses or the men, Hughes and Thompson called a halt to the expedition, retraced their steps to the North Saskatchewan River and returned to Rocky Mountain House.

The journey to discover a transcontinental route had failed barely three weeks after it had begun.

1

The Early Years: 1770–1784

IT WAS SUMMER ON LAKE SUPERIOR, sometime in the early 1820s. A heavy gale with howling winds and pouring rain had forced astronomer and retired fur trader David Thompson and the ragged British survey team to stop paddling and take cover at Cape Gargantua on the rugged northeastern shore. The dark waters of Lake Superior were menacing, churning like a boiling cauldron.

Since 1817, Thompson had been Britain's surveyor and astronomer on the International Boundary Commission, which was tasked with travelling and surveying part of the route proposed by the British for the Canada-US boundary. It was gruelling work. They travelled long distances, fought nature, scrambled for food and looked for shelter wherever they could find it. For Thompson, the difficult conditions were reminiscent of his wilderness days, when, as a trader-adventurer, surveyor, explorer, mapmaker, astronomer and soldier-merchant, he had criss-crossed the vast hinterland of Canada and the northern US by canoe, horseback, snow-shoes, dogsled and on foot. Now in his fifties, when many men took an easier path in life, Thompson was at it again—this time working for the British government to define Canada's borders. But did he miss those days when he lived on the raw edge of the wilderness?

While waiting for the wicked Lake Superior storm to subside, the commission's medical officer and assistant secretary, Dr. John J. Bigsby, worked alongside Thompson in their small tent and got a rare glimpse into Thompson's memories of those days. Bigsby later wrote, "Our astronomer was sitting in the tent, over a map, when he suddenly dropped his pencil on paper. Looking up, I saw that the dim curtain of reverie had fallen before his eyes, and the lights and shadows of former years were playing over his hard features." After a time, Bigsby broke into Thompson's trance, asking him "what he was thinking of and where he had got to."

"Got to?" repeated Thompson mechanically. He then continued:

Why, if you must know, I was once more on the east flank of the Rocky Mountains, in my old pursuits, with my old companions— scenes and friends I shall never more see. People may fancy and may say what they like, but give me a gallop into the natural meadows, the glorious hunting-grounds of Central America [north- and mid–North America], with their clear skies and bracing airs. Let me wander over parks of bison, deer, and moose feeding promiscuously. Let me listen at the close of the day to the cries of wild creatures, as I sit on the door of my skin-tent—and to the loud whistle of the stag, the sullen, gong-like boom of the elk, the bellow of the bison, or the wolf-howl . . . Then comes the buffalo hunt! And the well-trained Indian horse! How beautiful to watch his motions, prepared for the chase, as he stands on a gentle rise, in full view of a herd of bison.

Thompson had left the fur trade in 1812, after 28 years. He retired as a wealthy man to Terrebonne (near Montreal) and later Williamstown, Ontario, reaping the benefits of his hard work as a wintering partner of the North West Company (NWC). During those 28 years—first with the Hudson's Bay Company (HBC) and then with the NWC—Thompson had travelled and explored more than 107,000 km (65,000 miles), equivalent to travelling twice around the Earth, and mapped 3.9 million square kilometres, equivalent to one-sixth of North America. And he had kept detailed journals covering most of that time. During his final years, he would use those journals to write his epic memoir, finally published as *David Thompson's Narrative of his Explorations in Western America*, considered one of the best early travel books and a fascinating chronicle of environment, history and culture.

Who would have thought that a man born, raised and

educated in the intellectual heart of London would become one of North America's iconic wilderness men and a great geographer, cartographer, naturalist, adventurer-explorer, writer, scientist and innovator?

The Early Fur Trade in North America

When Thompson was born in 1770, the fur-trading empire of the HBC had already been operating for 100 years in the northern lands of present-day Canada. The North American fur trade had started because of European demand for men's felt hats made from beaver pelts. The most luxurious pelts came from the cold, far northern regions of North America. The wearing of hats began in the 1300s, becoming popular about 100 years later. Men adopted the hat as a fashion item, but then it became a symbol of the wearer's social status. It symbolized authority, hierarchy and importance. And the bigger the hat, the higher one's status.

It was that market for northern beaver pelts that fuelled the fierce rivalry between the early English and French fur traders and led to the formation of one of the world's oldest commercial empires, the HBC. On May 2, 1670, King Charles II of England granted a Royal Charter to the new company, officially known as "The Governor and Adventurers Trading into the Hudson Bay." The charter was written on five sheepskin parchments, with over 7,000 words of handwritten text. The original proprietors included the king's cousin, Prince Rupert, and 17 other business associates.

The king gave the new company "sole possession of all the seas, waters, lakes and lands of the Hudson Bay and its drainage system." The real-estate windfall was a virtual subcontinent of 3.8 million square kilometres of land. Geographically, it extended from the unexplored regions of today's Labrador in the east to the Rockies in the west. It included present-day northern Quebec and Ontario, all of Manitoba, southern Saskatchewan, eastern Northwest Territories and land south of the 49th parallel, taking in much of Minnesota and North Dakota in today's United States.

By the 1770s, the HBC's fur-trade monopoly was being seriously challenged, particularly by the formation in 1774 of the Montreal-based NWC. Thompson was born into a time when the fur trade in North America was booming and highly competitive.

Thompson in England

David Thompson was born in London, England, on April 30, 1770, and given the Welsh name Dafydd ap Thomas. His parents, David and Ann Thompson, moved from Wales to the Westminster district of London before he was born. Two years after David's birth, his brother John was born on January 25, 1772. Then, just 33 days later, tragedy struck when the boys' father died, leaving his widow to raise the two young children.

Ann struggled to keep the family together and to make a good life for her sons. But just over five years after her husband's death, she made the difficult decision to place David in the Grey Coat Hospital of Westminster, a respected charity school established in 1698 for poor children in the heart of London. On April 29, 1777, the day before his seventh birthday, David was admitted to the school.

At the time, there were two main charity schools (called "hospitals") in London: the prestigious Christ's Hospital (known as the Blue Coat Hospital), established in 1553 near St. Paul's Cathedral, and the Grey Coat Hospital. Both schools aimed to give poor children an education, prevent "pauperism," ensure they could lead "good industrious lives" and create apprenticeship opportunities for boys, particularly with the HBC. In its first 100 years, Grey Coat Hospital sent 11 students to be apprentices with the HBC.

At Grey Coat, David learned to read and write, studied mathematics and navigation, read ancient tales from Persia and Arabia and modern works like *Robinson Crusoe* and *Gulliver's Travels*. Since the school was located in the heart of London, David became an avid urban explorer. During school holidays, he wandered around Westminster Abbey, reading the detailed monument inscriptions, while at other times he strolled to nearby places like London Bridge, Vauxhall, Spring Gardens and St. James's Park.

In December 1783, the HBC visited Grey Coat Hospital to recruit boys to apprentice as clerks at their company's remote posts located on Hudson Bay. Thompson was selected by the school's governors on December 30 to be one of the two students offered to HBC (the other, Samuel John McPherson, ran away after being selected).

Thompson was indentured by the HBC as an apprentice for seven years, one of the company's "Hudson's Boys." This meant he would receive no pay for the seven years of his term. Upon completion of the term, if his work was satisfactory, he would have a career with the HBC. His apprenticeship would begin at the isolated and forlorn fur-trade post of Churchill Factory on the west coast of Hudson Bay.

Thompson was ready for adventure, his imagination and wanderlust fuelled by reading tales of danger, challenge and survival in strange lands. Reading had sharpened his observation skills, piqued his curiosity and laid a foundation for his lifelong habit of making detailed notes. "Books in those days were scarce and dear," wrote Thompson in his memoirs. "Those which pleased us most were the Tales of the Genii, the Persian and the Arabian Tales, with Robinson Crusoe and Gulliver's Travels: these gave us many subjects for discussion and how each would behave on various occasions . . . With such an account of the several regions of the earth and on such credible authority, I conceived myself to have knowledge to say something of any place I might come to."

The Leaving
On May 29, 1784, 14-year-old Thompson said farewell to his mother and brother John, boarded the HBC ship *Prince*

Rupert and set sail from Gravesend on the Thames River, destined for Churchill Factory. The ship, under the command of Captain Joshua Tunstall, joined two other HBC vessels—the *Sea Horse* and *King George*—sailing to the bay that summer. Before heading out for the dangerous voyage across the ocean, the three ships had one port to visit first: Stromness in the Orkney Islands.

On their way to Stromness, Thompson got his first introduction to smugglers and scoundrels. At dawn on the third morning of their journey, a Dutch lugger (a small two- to three-masted boat with a four-cornered sail on each mast) was sighted about a half mile from the *Prince Rupert*. The crew seemed to know that it was selling contraband liquor, and as none of the officers or ship's crew had stocked up on liquor before leaving because of England's high prices, they were ready to make a deal with the liquor lugger.

Thompson later wrote, "A boat was directly lowered, and the gunner, a tall handsome young man, stepped into her with four men, they were soon on board of the lugger, a case of gin was produced, a glass tasted; approved, the dutchman was in a hurry, as he said a Revenue Cutter was cruising near hand, and he must luff off."

A guinea was paid for the case of nine square glass bottles, which were put into the boat. Each bottle was full, with the corks cut close to the neck of the bottle, except for the bottle that the gunner had tasted; it had a long cork. "It was taken out, a glass handed round and each praised it." But the ship's carpenter, a veteran seaman, was suspicious and wished to taste some of the other bottles. So the cork was drawn on another bottle, a glass filled and tasted—and spit out. It was sea water, and except for the first "sample" bottle, all the others were found also to be filled with sea water. The gunner had therefore paid a guinea for only "three half pints of gin." The liquor merchants on the Dutch lugger had scammed them.

However, not all ships on the high seas meant trouble. On the fourth morning, with the hills of Scotland "lying blue in the western horizon to the east of us about two miles," a deep-sea fishing boat came up beside the *Prince Rupert*. On board were six hardy-looking men, "sitting up to their knees in fish, for the boat was full of the various kinds they had caught." Captain Tunstall bought some halibut and skate in exchange for old rope that the fishermen wanted for fettels (rope handles) for their baskets and buckets. Thompson wrote, "Our captain, pleased with his bargain, told me to give them a hat full of biscuit," which he delivered in a broad-brimmed hat. "Pleased with the ruddy looks of them, I filled my hat as full as it could hold . . . the boat's crew were so pleased they told me to hand down a bucket, which they filled with fresh caught herrings."

Six days after leaving London, the three ships anchored at Stromness. It would be another three weeks before they received final instructions from the HBC. To Thompson, the barren landscape of treeless Stromness was a shock after living in London with its beautiful green spaces. "I could not help staring to see if [what] was before me was reality for I had never read of such a place."

Already an astute observer of his surroundings, one of the first things that young Thompson noticed was the laborious work of kelp gatherers and the dirty black fires of their kilns. Decades later, he recalled, "The sea weeds were collected by a number of Men and Women; their legs appeared red and swelled. The sea weeds were collected into baskets ... and as they carried it over rough rocky shore left by the ebb tide to the kilns, the sea water streamed down their backs."

The seaweed was dried on shore boulders, then burned in large, stone-lined, circular pits, the residue being referred to as kelp. The fires spewed acrid, dirty smoke that could turn day into night. Once the seaweed turned to liquid, it was raked, stirred and tended until it became a coagulated mass; then it was shipped south to England as powdery vegetable alkali, an essential ingredient in making glass and soap and for bleaching linen. Orkney kelp production peaked between 1770 and 1830. It took from 20 to 24 tons of seaweed to produce one ton of kelp.

According to Thompson, one night the kelpers defied Captain Tunstall's orders to put out the fires. The captain had invited the other captains and some Orkney gentlemen to dine with him. Just before dinner, a wind change brought the sulphurous smoke directly onto the ship. The captain ordered the kelpers to extinguish their kilns, but they refused.

He then threatened to smash their kilns with cannon-balls, but again they refused, replying, "You may as well take our lives as our means, we will not put them out." The captain made inquiries as to how much money the workers made and was told only 10 pence when the kilns burned well. In one last attempt to resolve the situation amicably, the captain offered each kelper one shilling to stop the fires. They accepted. The kilns were extinguished, and the captain's dinner party went ahead.

Thompson called the work of the kelp gatherers "hard, wet labour" and compared their joyless work, "where not even a whistle was heard," with the jovial, singing plough-boys of England. And he lamented that Orkney "was rock, with very little soil, everywhere loose stones that hurt my feet, not a tree to be seen" and pondered the lifestyle of the people who lived in their low, dark houses.

One afternoon, Thompson entered such a house with one of the ship's petty officers, who was looking to buy some liquor. Inside, sitting by the turf fire, was a man wearing a homespun blue coat. The officer asked him if he had an "anker keg of comfort" (equal to 32 litres of gin). The man said yes, they settled on a price and soon the gin was on board the *Prince Rupert*. Liquor, it seemed, was cheaper and better quality here in Orkney than in London.

After receiving their sailing orders by letter from London, the three HBC ships left Stromness on July 3 and headed out to the ocean. Closer to America, they passed several icebergs, but it was Hudson Strait, the 450-mile-long arm of the Atlantic Ocean in northeastern Canada, which presented their greatest challenge. Located between Nunavut's Baffin Island and northern Quebec, the strait links the ocean with Hudson Bay. The biggest obstacle for sailing ships was working through the float ice that came down from Foxe Channel. Ships also encountered fog, strong currents and rushing tidal streams with tides that could exceed 30 feet. If there was a wind, a captain had some control; if there was no wind, ships drifted along at risk of hitting massive ice floes. On this voyage, the strait was so full of ice that it took the convoy a month to pass through it. Once through the strait, the ships separated to head to their destinations. One went to Fort Albany and Moose Factory, another to York Factory and the third, the *Prince Rupert*, arrived at Churchill Factory on September 2.

As the *Prince Rupert* pulled anchor and set sail for her return voyage to England, Thompson felt the hard reality of his new life. Years later, he still vividly remembered the emotional scene. "While the ship remained at anchor, from my parent and friends it appeared only a few weeks' distance, but when the ship sailed and from the top of the rocks I lost sight of her, the distance became immeasurable and I bid a long and sad farewell to my . . . country, an exile for ever."

Thompson never returned to England, nor saw his mother again.

The Apprentice:
1784–1787

FOR 14-YEAR-OLD THOMPSON, the spartan landscape of Churchill Factory was a stark contrast to the life he had led in the heart of London, one of Europe's busiest cities. However, even in this remotest of places, he would soon learn there was a rich legacy of drama, adventure and history.

The existence of Churchill Factory was due in large part to a remarkable Chipewyan woman named Thanadelthur. On November 24, 1714, 70 years before Thompson's arrival, she had arrived at York Fort (later called York Factory), which was located 150 miles south of the Churchill Factory site. She had just escaped from the Cree, who had held her captive for a year. An intelligent young woman, she had greatly impressed York Fort's governor, James Knight, who had been looking for a way to promote peace between the warring tribes of the Cree and Chipewyan, who belonged to the Dene Nation. He listened carefully when she explained that her people feared the Cree because they had guns; therefore, the Chipewyans would not come to the bay to trade because they would have to cross into Cree territory. She told Knight she wanted to help him end the hostilities so that her people could enjoy the benefits of trade goods. The following summer, on June 27, a delegation left York Fort on a peace mission to the Chipewyans who lived in the Barrens north and west of Churchill. Led by the HBC's William Stuart, it was guided by Thanadelthur and accompanied by 150 Cree. Knight had instructed Thanadelthur to tell the Chipewyans he would build a fort at the foot of the Churchill River.

The expedition was a harrowing year-long venture on the tundra. Food was in short supply, conditions were hard, and in the end, most of the Cree abandoned the group, leaving only Stuart, Thanadelthur, the Cree captain and a dozen Cree. When the rest of the Cree refused to go any farther— fearing retribution for nine Chipewyans they had found murdered on a trail—Thanadelthur persuaded them to stay in camp and wait for 10 days. During that time, she would find her people and bring them back to negotiate peace. They agreed, and Thanadelthur went out alone over the Barrens. The men had almost given up hope of seeing her again when on the 10th day she came into camp with two emissaries and accompanied by over 100 Chipewyans. A passionate and skilful orator, Thanadelthur successfully negotiated a truce between the warring Cree and Chipewyans.

Thanadelthur was planning another mission when she became ill and died on February 5, 1717. In her short 25-year life, she had left her mark as an ambassador of peace who helped open the northern fur trade. As promised, Knight constructed Churchill River Post in 1717, about four miles from the mouth of the river.

A French Attack

In 1719, the Churchill post was renamed Prince of Wales Fort (though later it would also be known as Churchill Factory). Sixteen years later, a stone fortress was built on an island at the entrance to the Churchill River (near present-day Churchill, Manitoba). The bastioned fort was star-shaped with 90-metre-long walls that were three metres high and protected by 42 cannons. It took 40 years to complete and was the only large stone fort overlooking the Arctic Ocean.

Two years before Thompson arrived at Churchill, the stone fort was the scene of naval drama. On August 8, 1782, three French naval warships headed toward the isolated fort: the 74-gun warship *Sceptre* and two 36-gun frigates, *Arlee* and *Engageante*. All were under the command of Admiral Jean-Francois de Galaup, Comte de La Pérouse, a seasoned navigator who later became a renowned explorer of the

Left in ruins by a French naval attack in 1782, the massive star-shaped Prince of Wales Fort at the mouth of the Churchill River has been partially reconstructed and is now a National Heritage Site. H.07.72.02.06(27)©PARKS CANADA/R.E. BILL/1977

Pacific. His ships had left the Caribbean on a secret expedition: to sail north, enter Hudson Bay, pillage and destroy the HBC trading posts and, if possible, capture HBC ships and cargo. On board were several hundred seamen and soldiers of the Armagnac and Auxerrois regiments, artillery detachments with field guns, marines and naval artillery.

At the time, the officer in charge of the Prince of Wales Fort was the northern explorer-trader Samuel Hearne. He had calmly watched, but done nothing as the French commander sent a reconnaissance boat up the river. The following day, the massive power of the French was on the move as hundreds of French soldiers landed and marched directly toward the fort.

Hearne's men wanted to put up a good fight and supposedly had "begged of Mr. Hearne to allow them to mow down the French Troops with the heavy guns loaded with grape shot." Hearne had refused. Instead, he ordered the gates to be opened, went out to meet the French and surrendered unconditionally without a shot being fired.

The French then stripped the fort of goods, supplies and furs, spiked the cannons, mined the walls and rampart and blew up the buildings. Hearne and his men were taken as prisoners. The French flotilla then continued on to York Fort and Fort Severn, where they repeated their depredations. After looting and reducing all three forts to rubble, the French left Hudson Bay at the beginning of September.

During the French attack, the three annual HBC supply ships had entered Hudson Bay, and two had spotted the foreign marauders. *Prince Rupert*, headed for Churchill under the command of Captain William Christopher, sighted the French flotilla on August 12. His ship was chased by one of the war frigates, but managed to escape. Captain Christopher then hid the *Prince Rupert* in Knapp's Bay until August 27. *King George III*, anchored at York Fort, had also sighted the French ships. She quickly finished loading the annual cargo of furs and safely departed for England. On August 29, the *Prince Rupert* sailed cautiously near Prince of Wales Fort at the entrance to the Churchill River, made the customary arrival signal (a cannon shot), but when there was no response from the smoldering ruins, she sailed on to England.

Released by the French, Hearne returned to Churchill River the following year with a 33-member crew to re-establish the post, selecting a site about four miles upriver. Thompson would have passed the stone fort's ruins as he sailed up the Churchill River. It was a compelling reminder of the isolation, desolation and vulnerability of his new home.

Churchill Factory

Hearne was still the post's governor when Thompson landed at Churchill on September 3, 1784. He had been instructed by the HBC's London committee to "keep [the] young apprentice busy with clerical duties and business of the fur trade" and to keep him away from factory servants, "the clannish illiterate Orkneymen."

Fall was a pleasant time in the subarctic tundra. The only biting insects left were the sandflies and midges, but they were soon gone, as were the migrating birds. By mid-October, snow was on the ground, the marshes and swamps were frozen and ice was forming on the rivers and along the seashore. By mid-November, the Churchill River had frozen over.

By late December, snow had drifted over the post's 12-foot stockades. In the yard, snow was six to ten feet deep, through which "avenues had to be cut and cleared of about four feet in width." For six months, beginning at the end of

October, everyone used snowshoes to get around. Thompson later wrote that it was "a long gloomy severe winter."

According to Thompson, all movements were for "self-preservation" in the intense cold. He wrote, "All the wood that could be collected for fuel gave us only one fire in the morning and another in the evening; the rest of the day, if bad weather, we had to walk in the guard room with our heavy coats of dressed Beaver." The inside walls of the two-storey residence were covered with four-inch-thick "rime," or hoarfrost, a coat of ice that helped to insulate the house.

Thompson had little work to do. The fort's trade had decreased significantly because fewer Natives were coming there, either to trade or get goods on credit. The primary reasons for this loss of trade were the slow recovery from the French attacks, increased competition from the rival Montreal-based fur traders and the effects of the 1782–83 smallpox epidemic, which had killed 9 out of 10 people in some northern First Nation communities.

As apprentice clerk, Thompson's job was to write, but only Hearne and officers had writing paper. "On my complaining that I should lose my writing for want of practice, Mr. Hearne employed me a few days on his manuscript, entitled 'A Journey to the North' [*A Journey from Prince of Wales's Fort in Hudson's Bay to the Northern Ocean*] and at another time I copied an Invoice." Thompson described Hearne as "a handsome man of six feet in height, of a ruddy complexion and remarkably well made, enjoying good health."

Since Hearne did not seem to have time for Thompson, three of the company's officers tried to keep him occupied: Deputy Governor Jefferson, Captain Thomas of the HBC sloop *Churchill* and surgeon John Toogood Hodges. "They had books, which they freely lent to me, among them were several on history and on animated Nature, these were what I paid most attention to as the most instructive." Thompson also learned valuable wilderness skills, including how to hunt grouse and kill them cleanly by putting the bird's head in his mouth and snapping its neck with his teeth.

However, for the most part, he wasn't using his educational skills. He wrote, "For all I had seen on their service neither writing nor reading was required, and my only business was to amuse myself, in winter growling at the cold, and in the open season shooting Gulls, Ducks, Plover and Curlews, and quarreling with Musketoes and Sand flies."

During summer, Thompson detested with passion the "myriads of tormenting Musketoes; the air is thick with them, there is no cessation day nor night of suffering from them . . . The narrow windows were so crowded with them they trod each other to death, in such numbers, we had to sweep them out twice a day." He noted there was only one remedy for them: to frequently apply sturgeon oil, which the Natives rubbed on themselves. He told of a sailor rubbing tar on his face, but the pesky insects stuck to it. Thompson concluded, "Oil is the only remedy."

Nonetheless, he was curious about the mosquitoes and

wondered, "Where and how do they pass the winter." He noted, "It is a curious fact the further to the northward, the more . . . numerous are all those flies." Having been influenced greatly by his reading while at Grey Coat, Thompson playfully later wrote, "Hudson's Bay is certainly a country that Sinbad the Sailor never saw, as he makes no mention of Musketoes."

York Factory

Thompson spent a year at desolate Churchill Factory before being assigned to York Factory, located on the left bank of the Hayes River, about five miles upriver. First built by the HBC in 1682 and expanded between 1714 and 1782, York Factory was the company's largest and most profitable post, although its trade had declined since the 1770s.

For 15-year-old Thompson, getting from Churchill to York Factory was an adventure in itself. He would have to walk the 150 miles to the post, accompanied by two of the post's packet Indians, who couriered letters and packages between the bay posts. The trek started on a windy September 4, 1785, when Hearne sent the trio out in the sloop to be dropped off at Cape Churchill, 36 miles southeast of the mouth of the river. Each was given a gun and one big blanket but no provisions, as they were expected to live off the land.

Before they left on the sloop, someone had given the two guides some grog. Once they were dropped off, the two guides got drunk and went to sleep, leaving Thompson to spend the day alone in the tundra. As he always did, the inquisitive Thompson kept himself busy by observing what was around him. He pondered questions like why ducks, geese and swans fly with such precision from northern breeding grounds to winter havens in Florida, Mississippi and the Gulf of Mexico. His Native guides told him the birds were guided by a manitou, a spirit that protected the flock.

It was a gruelling journey. Thompson slept on the ground wrapped in a blanket. Many days, they walked from morning to night without breakfast or dinner. Each day, they passed an average of 12 to 15 polar bears, lying in groups of 3 to 5 on the marsh close to shore, their heads together, bodies lying out from the centre like the spokes of a wheel. Thompson's companions told him this was a common sight. They also told him to "walk past them with a steady step without seeming to notice them."

On the sixth day, they crossed a deep brook, where on the opposite side was a large polar bear eating a beluga whale. Thompson later wrote, "We boldly took the ford thinking the Bear would go away, but when about half way across, he lifted his head, placed his fore paws on the Beluga, and uttering a loud growl, showed to us such a set of teeth as made us turn up the stream, and for fifty yards wade up to our middle before we could cross; during this time the Bear eyed us, growling like a Mastiff Dog."

Eleven days later, on September 15, the group arrived at

York Factory. The fort's governor at the time was 57-year-old Humphrey Marten, who had joined the HBC as a writer in May 1750. He had trained many apprentice clerks over the years and had no interest in doing it again. He ignored the written orders of May 4, 1785, sent to him by the HBC governor and committee based in London, England, which read, "As an Assistant Writer is much Wanted We have ordered our Apprentice David Thompson to be sent to you from Churchill: he has been instructed in the Mathematicks and writes a good Hand." Marten was also instructed to keep Thompson away "from the common Men and employed in the Writing accounts."

Instead, Marten assigned Thompson to live in the wild with a party of hunters to supply York Factory with fresh meat until spring. The party included three men (John Ballanden, Robert Tennant and a Native lad), a Native woman, four flat sleds and a large Newfoundland dog. The group left early on October 26, after the company boat dropped them off across the Hayes River on the frozen shore ice to hunt at French Creek.

Throughout the winter, Thompson would deliver meat to York Factory. On November 22, Thompson and Tennant returned with 15 rabbits, 60 pounds of fish, 30 grouse and 3 foxes. On December 23, Thompson came back with sleds loaded with 400 grouse, 48 rabbits, 52 marten, 3 foxes and 92 pounds of fish. A month later, Thompson brought in 300 grouse, followed by another 300 grouse two weeks after that.

However, his winter hunting days ended in mid-February when Governor Marten ordered him back to York Factory because he had frostbite on his face.

No matter what task he was given, young Thompson always remained an observer of his surroundings and took detailed notes. He saw winter's beauty in the fragile ice that blanketed nature. "A curious formation now takes place called Rime, of extreme thinness, adhering to the trees, willows, and every thing it can fasten on, its beautiful, clear, spangles forming flowers of every shape, of a most brilliant appearance, and the Sun shining on them, makes them too dazzling to the sight. Rime can only be formed in calm clear weather, and a gale of wind sweeps away all this magic scenery to be reformed on calm days. It appears to be formed of frozen dew." Later, he again commented on its beauty, saying that during clear days in the months of February and March, the "gaudy, spangled Rime is most brilliant, and requires a strong eye to look upon it."

Journey to the Interior

By Thompson's 16th birthday in 1786, he had survived the extremes of the subarctic, from the cold dark winters to hot, insect-infested summers. He had trekked the tundra, learned to kill grouse with his teeth, ice-fished on frozen rivers and tackled new skills like snowshoeing and paddling in the wild outback. In the summer of 1786, he would get hands-on endurance training in long-distance travel with the annual canoe brigade going inland. Assigned to the interior, Thompson was about to undertake a physically demanding journey, travelling eight weeks on ancient Aboriginal routes of long rivers, portages, rapids and lakes.

On July 22, 1786, a day after being outfitted with a trunk, handkerchief, shoes, shirts, a tin pot and cup, and a gun and powder, Thompson left York Factory in a 46-man canoe brigade. Their first stop would be Cumberland House, which had been established by Samuel Hearne in 1774 on Pine Island on the Saskatchewan River as the company's first inland post west of the bay.

In charge of the brigade was long-time trader Robert Longmore, the principal assistant to William Tomison, the chief inland governor of HBC in North America. Tomison had been appointed to succeed the retiring Marten as the governor of York Factory, though he would be supervising while residing inland, leaving Joseph Colen as York's resident chief. Later in the summer, Tomison left York and followed the brigade to the Saskatchewan River.

Tomison, born in 1739 at South Ronaldsay in Orkney, began his HBC career in 1760 as a labourer and worked for 51 years in what is now western Canada. He retired as a wealthy man in 1811 to South Ronaldsay, where he established and funded a school for poor children. An advocate for human equality, better treatment of employees and, like Thompson, against liquor as a trade item, Tomison was said to be a complex man, both generous and frugal. During the smallpox epidemic that raged among the Cree in western Canada in 1780–81, Tomison was in charge of Cumberland House and played a key role in assisting First Nations people. Realizing smallpox was contagious, Tomison quarantined those who were afflicted and used sulphur as a disinfectant. "Perhaps even more commendable is the remarkable compassion shown the Aboriginals by Tomison and his White employees. In their primitive and already crowded quarters at Cumberland House, Tomison's Caucasian HBC servants, under his direction, took in the dying Indians, provided them with food, shelter and 24 h care . . . and then, in most instances, dug their graves in deeply frozen ground in midwinter," writes Professor C. Stuart Houston and Dr. Stan Houston.

After leaving York Factory, the brigade paddled up the Hayes River against a strong current and spent many days "tracking," a technique used to pull canoes upriver when the water was either too swift or shallow to paddle. Long ropes were secured to the bow and stern of the canoe and then attached to harnesses put on men who pulled the canoe from shore. Another man stayed on the canoe to steer. The heat and incessant torment of hordes of mosquitoes made the job even more difficult. Hayes River has been called a "watery staircase," because of the numerous rapids and falls that require portaging. About 400 miles from York Factory, the end of the Hayes River is linked to the Echimamish River (Cree for "the river that flows both ways") by Painted Stone

Portage, an ancient Aboriginal spiritual site. Thompson commented that it was marked by a large manitou stone painted with red ochre, near which travellers usually laid offerings.

The Echimamish River took the brigade to the top of Lake Winnipeg, where they paddled 85 miles along the northern shore, down the western side to the mouth of the Saskatchewan River and two miles farther to the foot of Grand Rapids. There they hauled everything over a brutal two-mile portage to the head of the rapids.

Why was the HBC now sending its employees on such arduous journeys deep into the wilderness? It wasn't for exploration or to open the country for settlers; rather, it was strictly a business decision. The NWC was setting up trade posts deep in the fur-rich territories and encouraging the Natives to bring their furs to them. In other words, NWC was bringing the "store" to the Natives, whereas HBC had traditionally expected the Natives to travel long distances to the subarctic posts on Hudson Bay. To be competitive, HBC had to establish posts in the interior, and the Saskatchewan River was the road they would travel to get there.

Wintering on the Saskatchewan

After the brigade reached Cumberland House, 200 miles up the Saskatchewan River (near today's Manitoba–Saskatchewan border), they made a quick stop to take on dried provisions and then continued paddling, arriving on September 25 at the South Branch House site (near present-day Batoche, Saskatchewan). They started clearing the site a week later. When Tomison visited on October 17 to check progress, he found that "Some [were] building the Chimneys, some putting the roof on the House, some making Mortar for the Chimneys, some carrying Stones." By December 20, they had completed building the house.

Built in the simple, sturdy Greek Doric style, the cabin was 36 feet long, 20 feet wide and 7 feet high with a split-log roof, the outside mudded and covered with earth. Thompson later wrote, "The two chimneys were built of mud, mixed with chopped coarse grass, the floors were of split logs. The house [was] divided into three by walls of logs, with doors cut in them, one of twelve feet by twenty for the goods, furs and provisions, ten feet for a hall for business and trading with the Indians, the other fourteen feet for the men called the guard room. The Indian hall was occupied by Mr. Oman and myself."

In charge of South Branch House was Mitchell Oman, a "stout and rough" Orcadian who joined the HBC in 1771 as a labourer at York Factory. He had been present at the infamous 1783 attack by the French, but had escaped. As he couldn't read or write, and signed his documents with an x, he had others, like Thompson, write the post journals for him.

On May 30, 1787, Thompson left South Branch House with the annual canoe brigade destined for York Factory, where their furs would be loaded on company ships heading for

England. Along the way, the group stopped at Cumberland House, where Tomison ordered Thompson to stay for the summer. It was a great training opportunity for the apprentice clerk, as he learned new skills such as fishing with nets, making and repairing fishnets, and how to extract oil (used to light the post's lamps) from a sturgeon.

In his absence, Tomison had left the post under the direction of George Hudson, a former student of Grey Coat Hospital who, like Thompson, had been an indentured apprentice. However, rather than camaraderie, Thompson had much disdain for Hudson. "He had been here about thirteen years, had lost all his education, except reading and writing, and the little of this, for the accounts of the trade appeared labor to him; he appeared in a state of apathy, always smoking tobacco mixed with weed, had no conversation with any person, the little business he had was done with few words and [he] took no exercise. I was sadly disappointed in him," wrote Thompson.

Thompson stayed the winter at the post, filling his days playing draughts, an ancient board game similar to American checkers. "It is a game of skill and I became an expert at it," he wrote, adding that the post had two checkerboards. "Having nothing to do, it was my constant employment, and for want of a companion frequently played by myself."

It was during such a game that something bizarre happened. According to Thompson, "I was sitting at a small table with the chequerboard before me, when the devil sat down opposite to me, his features and color were those of a Spaniard. He had two short black horns on his forehead, which pointed forwards, his head and body down to the waist (I saw no more) was covered with glossy, black, curling hair, his countenance mild and grave. We began playing [and] played several games and he lost every game, kept his temper, but looked more grave; at length he got up, or rather disappeared."

Thompson was stunned. It was broad daylight, and he knew he wasn't asleep, yet he asked himself, "Was it a dream, or was it a reality. I could not decide." He did know, however, that it had been a life-altering moment. From that day forward, he resolved "never to play a game of chance, or skill, or any thing that had the appearance of them." The incident left such an indelible mark on him that even while writing his memoirs 63 years later, he could recall it in great detail.

From Fur Trader to Surveyor: 1787–1791

FROM THE BEGINNING OF THE HBC in 1670, the company's fur-trading empire had been built on the business model of the First Nations people transporting their furs to trade for goods and provisions at the posts on Hudson Bay. Each summer, HBC supply ships would deliver trade goods from England to the bayside posts and return to England with cargoes of furs, mainly beaver pelts. Because the First Nations people journeyed to the posts, the HBC men seldom ventured inland. They had no reason to travel—they waited for the furs to come to them.

However, from the 1770s onward, the Montreal-based fur traders had set up posts in the rich fur regions of the interior, drawing trade away from the HBC. The First

Nations people, experienced and sharp traders, now had the option of trading their furs without making the long canoe trek to Hudson Bay. The original 100-year-old operational plan of the HBC was becoming outdated.

When the Montreal-based partners banded together in 1774 to form the NWC, the HBC had to change their operations dramatically. For the first time in 100 years, the governors decided to build trading posts inland and compete directly with the NWC. They had to get to know the First Nations people, create alliances and build a customer base. The first inland post, Cumberland House, was established on the Saskatchewan River in 1774, and a second one, Hudson House, five years later in 1779.

By the time Thompson arrived at Churchill Factory, the rival NWC already had a network of trading posts on the Saskatchewan River, in the territory south of York and Churchill factories and in the Athabasca region. Tomison reported in 1786 that in the Saskatchewan area alone, there were already 180 French traders and the same number in the Athabasca country. The HBC sent more men to the interior, but the following year Tomison still only had 44 men, including Thompson, to compete against the NWC.

One of the strategies Tomison initiated to counter NWC influence was to develop Native alliances by sending his men to winter with members of the Blackfoot Confederacy, which consisted of three Algonquin-speaking tribes, the Blackfoot (Siksika), Blood (Kainai) and Peigan (Piikani). Living with the First Nations people was an immersion program for the future fur traders; they learned the language, customs and culture of the people and established direct trade links.

A Peigan Winter

In early September 1787, after spending the summer at Cumberland House, Thompson accompanied Tomison (who had returned from the annual brigade to York) up the Saskatchewan and North Saskatchewan rivers to Manchester House (near present-day North Battleford, Saskatchewan). Tomison had selected Thompson to be part of a six-member trading group to winter with the Peigan camped near the Bow River at the foothills of the Rockies. Veteran trader John Gaddy, who had already spent the two previous winters with the Peigan, would lead the group. Thompson was paired with an Orkney lad, William Flett.

The Peigan, a nomadic people who were great horsemen and warriors, controlled an area extending from the foothills of the Rockies eastward to the present Alberta–Saskatchewan border, and from the North Saskatchewan River south to the Missouri River in today's Montana. Much of the buffalo-hunting grounds of the plains fell within their territory.

For his winter's stay with the Peigan, Thompson's cloth-ing consisted of two shirts, a blue cloth jacket, leather pants and coat, a blanket and a bison robe. While living with the Peigan, the men could carry on trading for themselves, using goods advanced to them by the HBC. Each man had two horses to carry his baggage, goods and self, except Thompson, who had only one horse. As a result, he walked most of the way to the Bow River, averaging 15 miles a day.

The group set off at the end of September and were met a month later by a dozen armed Peigan warriors a few miles past the Bow River. "They were well mounted, and armed with Bows and quivers of arrows," Thompson later wrote. "They gave us a hearty welcome, told us to camp where they met us, and would soon bring us some good cow meat, and next morning show us to the camp. Awhile after sunset they brought us two horse-loads of fat cow meat, we were hungry, and sat up part of the night roasting and eating; as it was a long month since we had a good meal. Two of them passed the night with us and were as anxious for news as any people could be."

The next morning, more Peigan arrived to escort Thompson and his group to their camp. Thompson noted, "All the elderly men came and gave us their left hand and said they were thankful we had come, as they were in want of ammunition and tobacco. We separated ourselves two by two to three different tents where the most respectable men lived. William Flett and myself were lodged in the tent of an old man, whose hair was grey with age, his countenance grave, but mild and open; he was full six feet in height, erect, and of a frame that shewed strength and activity."

The Peigan elder was Saukamappee, a respected warrior now around 85 to 90 years of age; his teepee would be Thompson's home for the winter. After a few days, Saukamappee spoke to Thompson in the Cree language, asking him if he understood it and how long it had been since he had left his own country. Thompson replied that yes, because he traded with the Cree, he could "speak their tongue sufficient for common purpose" and that this was his fourth winter since leaving England.

Saukamappee smiled. He seemed to understand the young lad's feelings about exile from his home country, because he too was far away from his homeland. Saukamappee told Thompson that he was not a Peigan at all, but a Cree from the Pasquiaw River (about 50 miles below Cumberland House). "It is many winters since I last saw the ground where my parents lie. I came here as a young man, and my name is still the same I then received."

The elder inquired of Thompson about the people and news of his native land, after which the elder fell silent, then said, "What a stranger I now find myself in the land of my fathers."

Thompson later wrote, "Almost every evening for the time of four months I sat and listened to the old man, without being in the least tired ... blended with the habits, customs and manners, politics and religion such as it was, [were] anecdotes of the Indian chiefs and the means of their gaining influence in war and peace ... I always found something to interest me."

In January, a large Peigan war party arrived at the camp, and their war chief, Kootanae Appee, came to visit his friend Saukamappee. On entering the tent, Kootanae Appee offered his left hand to Thompson, who gladly responded by extending to the chief his right hand for a handshake. The war chief looked sharply at him, but then smiled. Kootanae Appee talked with the Peigan elder for about half an hour, during which time Saukamappee received the war chief's assurance he would provide Thompson with protection.

Thompson described Kootanae Appee as being "about forty years of age, and his height between six feet two to four inches; more formed for activity than strength, yet well formed for either; his face a fine oval, high forehead and nose somewhat aquiline; his large black eyes, and countenance were open, frank, but somewhat stern; he was a noble specimen of the Indian Warrior of the great plains." When Kootanae Appee left the tent, Thompson again extended his right hand in a friendly farewell handshake. Years later, the two men would meet again in less pleasant circumstances.

When they were alone, Saukamappee explained to the 17-year-old Thompson how his response to the extended left hand of a Peigan could be viewed as an insult or a challenge, particularly to those who had never before met a white man. "If one of our people offers you his left give him your left hand, for the right hand is no mark of friendship. This hand wields the spear, draws the Bow, and the trigger of the gun; it is the hand of death. The left hand is next to the heart, and speaks truth and friendship, it holds the shield of protection, and is the hand of life," said Saukamappee. The respected elder died five years later, in 1793, after a leg infection from a beaver bite.

Thompson and the others left the Peigan camp four months later and returned to Manchester House. He was warmly greeted by Tomison, although the older man did not like the young lad's bedraggled appearance and promptly ordered the post's tailor to make Thompson a new jacket.

The Turning Point

Once the rivers became clear of ice, Tomison again led the canoe brigade of furs to York Factory. However, he sent Thompson to Hudson House for the summer, along with 6 others and about 40 HBC horses. Thompson, who kept the Hudson House journals from May 24 to September 19, 1788, later wrote, "We had at least four months to pass with barely a month's dried provisions, and for the rest we had to hunt the Bison and Deer, which we thought rather an honor than a hardship." Though the horses and their keepers were back about five miles in the forest, Thompson and a companion would go hunting and exploring on horseback every couple of days.

In early September, Tomison returned from York Factory and headed to Manchester House, ordering Thompson and four others to bring the horses. Life at Manchester House settled into a slow-paced routine, with Thompson noting, "Winter came on and affairs went on as usual." But on December 23, a terrible accident changed the course of Thompson's life.

The day had started with the normal fur-trade activities.

One party of men, including Thompson, had been sent out to cut firewood, while another returned with nine sleds full of meat from the hunter's tent. In the early evening, Thompson was hauling a sled-load of cut firewood along the riverbank about a mile from Manchester House. Suddenly he slipped and fell down the bank of the North Saskatchewan River, breaking his leg. Thompson screamed in agony as the others lifted him into a canoe as gently as they could and paddled him back to the post.

Tomison's journal entry of December 23 read, "David Thompson unfortunately fell coming down the River Bank about one Mile from the House by which his leg caught between a stick and the Sled which fractured the bone and otherwise bruised his leg very much. I set it and put splinters around it with bandages in the best manner I could but such accidents would require a more skilful Person than I am."

It was a life-threatening injury—a broken femur in his right leg that initially required 24-hour care. Tomison's journal entries chronicled Thompson's slow recovery. On January 12, 1789, he wrote, "David Thompson so far recovered as not to want any attendance at night." The March 29 entry reads, "David Thompson was out of bed today for the first time but had not set long before his foot and ankle swelled a good deal so that he was obliged to lie down again . . . God only knows how it may turn out." Five weeks later, he wrote, "David Thompson's leg I am afraid will turn out to be a mortification as the joint of his ankle has never lowered of the swelling."

Tomison cared deeply about the well-being of his young apprentice clerk, who later wrote, "Mr. Tomison behaved with the tenderness of a father to me and alleviated my sufferings all he could."

On May 17, Thompson was brought by stretcher to a canoe loaded with luggage and taken to Cumberland House. "By his own desire, I am taking David Thompson down but God knows what will come of him," wrote Tomison. Thompson remained at Cumberland House during the summer of 1789 under the care of the post's manager, Malcolm Ross.

Although the accident had brought Thompson to the brink of death, it became a turning point in his life. He later wrote, "Coming down a rude steep bank I fell and broke the large bone of my right leg and had to be hauled home, which by the mercy of God turned out to be the best thing that ever happened to me."

The accident and long convalescence had placed Thompson in the right place at the right time and would set him on the path to becoming one of North America's greatest surveyors and geographers. And it was all because of the arrival at Cumberland House of the HBC's chief surveyor, the articulate Philip Turnor.

An Excellent Master of the Science

On October 7, 1789, Philip Turnor arrived to winter at Cumberland House and plan his expedition to Lake Athabasca the following year. He was accompanied by his assistant, George Hudson. Thompson wrote, "This was a fortunate arrival for me, as Mr. Turnor was well-versed in mathematics, was one of the compilers of the nautical Almanac, and a practical astronomer."

Appointed in 1778 as the company's first official surveyor, Turnor had already visited most of the HBC posts, calculated their latitude and longitude and determined the distances between them. He had also been in charge of Brunswick House in 1782 and established a new post on the Abitibi River in 1784. Turnor had spent the past two years compiling maps in London. While there, he had advised the HBC's governing committee that to stay competitive, the company would have to find a route to the fur-rich Lake Athabasca area. The committee in London agreed and sent Turnor back to Rupert's Land to find and survey that route, an assignment he said would shape the future of the HBC.

Turnor, however, wouldn't be the first European in the Athabasca area; that honour went to NWC trader Peter Pond in 1778–79. Pond reached Lake Athabasca by heading up the Churchill River to Île-à-la-Crosse Lake, then northwest over the rugged 12-mile Methye Portage, which led to river systems flowing into Lake Athabasca. In 1786, Pond was charged with murdering a trader named Jean-Étienne Waddens at Île-à-la-Crosse and was subsequently removed from the region. However, each spring, canoes from the NWC laden with furs from the Athabasca area continued to head back to the company's headquarters at Grand Portage;

Cumberland House, the HBC's first inland post, was established in 1774 on the Saskatchewan River by Samuel Hearne. It was sketched by John Fleming in 1858. JOHN FLEMING

from there, the furs were taken to the fur merchants in Montreal for sale in Europe. Over half of the NWC's profits are estimated to have come from furs that travelled over the Methye Portage.

As an apprentice clerk, Thompson was not allowed to participate in the dinner-table conversations between Turnor and the officers, but he listened and learned. He was intrigued by the survey instruments—how they were used to study the skies and calculate geographical landmarks—and curious about how coordinates were used to produce a map.

While mentoring Thompson in surveying and astronomy skills, Turnor allowed the young man to use his instruments to make observations. Thompson wrote, "Under him, I regained my mathematical education and during winter became his only assistant, thus learning practical astronomy under an excellent master of the science." Practical astronomy was based on the technological advances of the time, like the 1757 invention of the sextant and the development of precise, reliable watches. Thompson made his first navigational recording on February 1, 1790; in the next four months, he made 34 lunar-distance measurements for longitude and six observations for latitude. Turnor felt the young apprentice an excellent candidate to be a surveyor and mapmaker for the HBC.

On April 19, the 29-year-old Hudson suddenly died and was buried at Cumberland House. Thompson felt he was the most qualified candidate to become Turnor's new assistant surveyor on the Athabasca expedition. However, because Thompson's broken leg was still healing and he was suffering from vision problems due to an eye infection, Turnor selected Peter Fidler for the position. Fidler would later go on to become the HBC's chief surveyor.

On June 9, disappointed but still passionate about surveying, Thompson accompanied the canoe brigade to York Factory. Along the way, he surveyed the route using Turnor's sextant. After a short stay at York Factory, where he met up with his brother, John, now working for the HBC, Thompson returned to Cumberland House to spend the winter of 1790–91.

4

Travels in the North: 1792–1797

FROM 1792 TO 1797, THOMPSON criss-crossed the hinterland from the bayside factories on Hudson Bay to the inland fur-trading posts via a network of lakes, rivers and portages, logging an incredible number of miles by canoe, horse, dog-sled, snowshoes and on foot. Wherever he went, he carried along his survey instruments, papers and books, so he could take astronomical observations for latitude and longitude and log the measurements in his journals and field notes.

While at York Factory during the spring of 1792, Thompson witnessed a remarkable event when he went hunting with two others up the Nelson River. "The weather cold and uncomfortable, we were sitting by our fire, when we heard a noise as of distant thunder, and somewhat alarmed, put our four guns and blankets into the canoe and sat quietly in it, waiting what it could be; with surprise we heard the sound increasing and rushing towards us, but we were not long in suspense. About forty yards below us, a vast herd of Rein Deer [caribou] . . . [came] rushing through the woods; we waited to see this vast herd pass." The herd continued to pass until sunset, and the next day, another "dense herd" came crashing through. Thompson determined that over 3.5 million caribou passed by them in those two days. Natives said the massive herd was under direct orders of Manitou, and after discussions, Thompson admitted, "I had to give up the idea of my doctrine of Instinct to that of their Manitou."

On September 5, 1792, Thompson and his friend William Hemmings Cook left York Factory with two canoes and reached the Saskatchewan River 25 days later. Cook and his canoe turned up the Grass River to Chatham House, which he had established the year before on Wintering Lake. Thompson continued paddling down the Saskatchewan River until October 8, when he arrived at a rocky point on the west side of Sipiwesk Lake and built the small trading post, Seepaywisk House.

During the winter, food was scarce, forcing Thompson to snowshoe on several occasions to Cook's Chatham House for provisions, a 60-mile return trip. Each time he ventured out, he continued to take astronomical readings, recording 28 lunar observations that winter.

In the spring of 1793, when the river was clear of ice, Thompson left Seepaywisk House, crossed Wintering Lake, went up the Burntwood River and travelled across Duck Portage to ascend 33 miles up the Churchill River. He intended to reach Reindeer Lake; however, his guides failed to meet him, so Thompson paddled on to York Factory.

After a few weeks, Thompson was off again, travelling to Cumberland House, South Branch House and Manchester House on his way to Buckingham House (near present-day St. Paul, Alberta) on the North Saskatchewan River. He did a quick trip on horseback to Beaver Hills, returning on November 29 to winter at Buckingham House, which was under the charge of his old friend and caregiver Tomison. On May 16, 1794, Thompson left Buckingham House on the annual canoe brigade to York Factory, surveying the river as he went along.

Barely two months after Thompson passed South Branch House on his way to York, the post was the site of a brutal attack by the Gros Ventre (also called Fall Indians and today known as Atsina). The problems had begun the previous summer, when, according to the NWC's Duncan McGillivray, a band of Woodland Cree attacked a 16-lodge camp of Gros Ventre, their long-time enemies, near South Branch and "like hungry Wolves and with remorseless fury butchered them all in cold blood except a few children whom they preserved for Slaves." Fear of the Crees kept the Gros Ventre from retaliating; instead, they took out their revenge on the European traders who had furnished the Cree with weapons.

Most of the HBC men from South Branch House were away on their annual trip to York Factory on the fateful July day when about 100 Gros Ventre warriors arrived on horseback at South Branch House. The Gros Ventre set fire to the stockade and then entered the post. Of the four men remaining that day at South Branch, three were killed and scalped: W. Fea, H. Brough and post manager M. Annal. They also murdered Annal's Assiniboine wife and their two youngest children and abducted two young women. The sole survivor at the post was trader Cornelius Van Driel; he escaped the carnage by hiding for eight hours in a heap of rubbish in an abandoned open cellar. After destroying the HBC post, the Gros Ventre attacked the nearby NWC post, but the Nor'Westers successfully fought them, killing their war chief, L'Homme de Callumet, and four warriors and wounding nine others.

Thompson had been at York Factory when the attack occurred, but had left before news of it arrived there. Paddling up the Nelson and Grassy rivers, he reached Reed Lake House in early September and spent the winter there with Malcolm Ross, trading, surveying and taking 46 lunar-distance observations for longitude.

By July 5, 1795, Thompson and Ross were back at York Factory with five canoe-loads of furs. Thirteen days later, they ascended the Nelson River and on September 6, arrived at Duck Portage on the west end of Sisipuk Lake. Here the men divided up the trade goods, and Ross continued upriver with three canoes to build Fairford House, near the confluence of the Churchill and Reindeer rivers. Meanwhile, on the south side of Duck Portage, shortly after Thompson and his four men built a trading post, a rival Canadian trader arrived and put his house 30 yards to the east. In the middle of winter, with temperatures hovering between -32 and -45°C, additional traders came to compete with Thompson for the Native trade, but to his surprise, this time they were fellow HBC traders.

On January 12, 1796, five traders arrived from the HBC's Three Points Post, about a two-day journey from Duck Portage. In charge of the group was George Charles, an inland trader from Churchill Factory and Thompson's former schoolmate at Grey Coat Hospital. Charles had come to ask for assistance in collecting debts he said were owed to Churchill by Natives trading at Duck Portage. Thompson refused to help. Charles left two days later, but three of his men remained in the area for the winter, trading in competition with Thompson. They worked under the authority of the governor of Churchill, whereas Thompson worked under York Factory. At the time, HBC's fur trade was divided into districts, administered by a governor at one of the factories along Hudson Bay.

In the spring, a furious Thompson complained to York council, "I cannot help being of the opinion that they . . .

consider themselves of a different interest and have accordingly privately opposed us to their utmost."

Reaching Lake Athabasca

Thompson's anger over the rival traders soon dissipated when he made his first survey eastward to the mouth of the Kississing River, followed by a survey of the Churchill River to Ross' Fairford House, arriving there on May 27. Waiting at the post were two Chipewyan guides who were to accompany him on his expedition to find a shorter, more direct route to the east end of Lake Athabasca from Churchill River, bypassing the existing route via Île-à-la-Crosse and Methye Portage.

The two guides, Kozdaw and Paddy, were seasoned bushmen, although their experience in Athabasca was limited to winter hunting. Kozdaw was a powerful man, active and "ready for every kind of service . . . under all the wildness was a kind and faithful heart." Paddy was slender, thoughtful and mild-mannered. After constructing a 17-foot birchbark canoe, the trio left Fairford House on June 10, paddled 64 miles up the Reindeer River and coasted 80 miles on Wollaston Lake before reaching the head of Black River, which discharged into the eastern end of Lake Athabasca.

Thompson's mission was accomplished on July 2 when they arrived at the eastern end of Lake Athabasca (the lake itself had already been surveyed by Turnor in 1791). The three men turned the canoe around and headed back to Reindeer Lake on what was supposed to be an easy return trip. Halfway up the Black River, however, they ran into such hardship that Thompson at one point told his companions, "Leave me to my fate." It began when Kozdaw and Paddy were tracking the canoe with Thompson seated inside to steer it. The guides stopped to argue about the placement of the tracking line. Meanwhile, the current was carrying the canoe away from the shore into midstream and at the same time swinging it uncontrollably from side to side. Thompson frantically waved at the two men to let go of the rope. "I called for them to go on. They could not hear me for the noise of the fall. I then waved my hand for them to proceed, meanwhile the current was drifting me out. And having only one hand to guide the canoe, the Indians standing still, the canoe took a sheer across the current. To prevent the canoe upsetting, I waved my hand to them to let go the line and leave me to my fate, which they obeyed," wrote Thompson.

Thompson sprung to the bow of the canoe and cut the line with his pocket knife. "By this time I was on the head of the fall; all I could do was to place the canoe to go down bow foremost. In an instant the canoe was precipitated down the fall (twelve feet), and buried under the waves. I was struck out of the canoe, and when I arose among the waves, the canoe came on me and buried [me] beneath it; to raise myself I struck my feet against the rough bottom and came up close to the canoe, which I grasped, and being now on shoal water, I was able to conduct the canoe to the shore."

Nothing remained in their capsized canoe except for their tent, axe and pewter basin. Thompson lay on the rock, bruised and exhausted, while Kozdaw and Paddy went along the shore to see what they could recover. A half hour later, they returned with the paddles and Thompson's cork-lined box with his sextant, survey instruments and papers. Thompson later wrote, "We had no time to lose . . . we divided the small tent into three pieces to wrap around ourselves, as a defence against the flies in the day, and something to keep us from the cold at night, for the nights are always cold."

His companions repaired the canoe with "Gum from the Pines," and a fire was started using the steel blades of Thompson's pocket knife. According to Thompson, the group was in bad shape. "Our destitute condition stared us in the face . . . [a] long journey through a barren country without provisions, or the means of obtaining any, almost naked, suffering from the weather." He later wrote that by July 16, "both Paddy and I were now like skeletons . . . we thought it useless to go any further but die where we were." However, though weak, they got back in the canoe and in the afternoon met a couple of Chipewyans, who provided them with food and provisions to continue their journey.

Thompson and the guides arrived back at Fairford House on July 21. A month later, Ross returned from York Factory with four small canoes carrying a total of about 2,400 pounds of trade goods for the winter. During his stay at York Factory, the 41-year-old Ross had submitted his request to retire from the HBC in 1797, giving the required one-year notice to the London committee. To fill his position of Master to the Northward, which carried the responsibility of managing a successful fur trade, Ross noted in his journal on September 5 that Thompson had been "appointed by the Council at York to take charge next year when I shall resign."

As historian Richard Glover notes, Thompson's promotion changed the relationship between him and Ross. Glover writes that Thompson "was heir apparent to a very important and responsible job; and for that reason Ross perhaps deferred more to the younger man than he might otherwise have done." That shift in power might have affected Ross' decision as to which route they should take on their fall trip back into the Athabasca country. Glover notes that Ross' preference, as indicated in his journal, was "the Isle Crosse Road" that he had already travelled with Turnor's expedition in 1790–92. But Thompson lobbied to take his recently discovered route to Athabasca, arguing that it was practicable with large canoes, even though Paint River, a small and shallow creek, would be on the route. Ross felt the creek would be even shallower in the fall, but Thompson disagreed, saying he had been informed that the creek would be even deeper in the fall. Against his better judgement, Ross agreed to take Thompson's new route.

Ross had been right. The Paint River was almost dried up in places, forcing the expedition to alternate between paddling short distances and portaging. On September 11, Ross finally convinced Thompson there was no point in continuing. The group turned around and headed back to Reindeer Lake, where they built a small log cabin, only 26 by 20 feet, which they called Bedford House. The wintering post accommodated 20 people, including two women and three children.

The expedition had gone badly. Thompson, the future Master to the Northward, had put the group in a difficult position. Ross wrote, "I am at a loss, how I shall winter so many people in such a poor Country . . . Had I gone by the Isle Crosse, I would not have been in any dread of wintering as many more as I have with me at present."

A Momentous Decision

Though it was an intensely cold winter on Reindeer Lake, Thompson marvelled at its beauty, particularly the aurora borealis. He wrote, "the whole heavens were in a bright glow . . . the Aurora was equally bright, sometimes, indeed often, with a tremulous motion in immense sheets, slightly tinged with the colors of the Rainbow, [and] would roll, from horizon to horizon." His inquisitive mind had many unanswered questions about the dancing lights. "What is the cause that this place seems to be in the centre of the most vivid brightness and extension of the Aurora; from whence this immense extent of electric fluid, how is it formed, whither does it go?"

Thompson spent the winter travelling, surveying, hunting and fishing around Reindeer Lake, which was 230 miles long and, in some places, 100 miles wide. On one trip, he got some tips on ice fishing from an old Chipewyan man. Thompson had cut five holes in the ice and caught nothing in two days, while in one hour the elder had pulled out a 30-pounder. He told Thompson to grease his bait and also advised that the best time for trout to take bait was noon, and only for a while after sunrise and near sunset.

On April 6, Ross and Thompson received a visitor, Alexander Fraser, a rival fur trader from the NWC. He had established a post at the mouth of the Reindeer River, south of Bedford House. Less than six weeks after Fraser's visit, Thompson made an unexpected announcement to Ross, who recorded the news in his journal entry for Sunday, May 21, 1797: "This morning Mr. David Thompson acquainted Me with his time being out with your Honours and thought himself a freeborn subject and at liberty to choose any service he thought to be most to his advantage and is to quit your service and enter the Canadian company's Employ."

Thompson had considered his HBC contract to be over on May 20 and believed that he would be a free agent the next day. This was not technically true, as Thompson had failed to adhere to the HBC policy of giving one year's notice of any leaving.

Why did Thompson suddenly leave the HBC and join the NWC? The question has intrigued historians. Some say he did not want the promotion to Master to the Northward because it might have limited the time available for his passions of surveying, astronomy and exploration. Others suggest the failed fall expedition may have undermined his co-workers' support and confidence in him. Or had Alexander Fraser offered him the job as the company's chief surveyor when he visited Bedford House in April? The reasons for Thompson's decision remain a mystery.

What historians do know is that at 2:30 a.m. on May 23, 1797, during a snowstorm, Thompson packed up his survey equipment, papers and belongings and snowshoed away from his HBC career. According to Thompson, "My time was up, and I determined to seek that employment from the Company Merchants of Canada, carrying on the Fur Trade, under the name of the North West Company. With two Natives I proceeded to their nearest trading House, under the charge of Mr. Alexander Fraser and by the usual route of the Canoes arrived at the Great Carrying Place on the north shore of Lake Superior, then the depot of the merchandise from Montreal; and of the Furs from the interior countries."

Cartographer and Thompson researcher Andreas (Andy) Korsos has calculated that Thompson travelled 18,728 kilometres during his 13 years of service with the HBC.

CHAPTER

A Remarkable Journey: 1797–1798

IN 1784—THE SAME YEAR that Thompson arrived at the HBC's Churchill Factory—the NWC formalized its partnership between the fur-trading merchants in Montreal and its traders in the field, and defined its organizational structure. At the top were the Montreal partners or agents, the wealthy men who controlled NWC. Predominantly Scottish, they raised capital, hired voyageurs, purchased trade goods and marketed the furs.

American author Washington Irving, who socialized with the Montreal partners, described the fur barons:

The partners from Montreal ... were the lords of the ascendant; coming from the midst of luxurious and ostentatious life, they quite eclipsed their compeers from the woods, whose forms and faces had been battered and hardened by hard living and hard service, and whose garments and equipment were all the worse for wear. Indeed, the partners from below considered the whole dignity of the company as represented in their persons, and conducted themselves in suitable style. They ascended the rivers in great state, like sovereigns making a progress: or rather like Highland chieftains navigating their subject lakes. They were wrapped in rich furs, their huge canoes freighted with every convenience and luxury, and manned by Canadian voyageurs, as obedient as Highland clansmen. They carried up with them cooks and bakers, together with delicacies of every kind, and abundance of choice wines for the banquets which attended this great convocation.

At the second level were the wintering partners who lived year-round in the interior. They managed the trading activities in a region, negotiated directly with the First Nations and supervised traders in their districts. Each wintering partner would be in charge of large areas known as districts; each district would be divided into several departments, and each department included several wintering posts. No one could be a partner without first spending time in the wilderness.

At the third level were the company clerks. They managed the small fur posts and kept the posts' daily record of activities. The guides and interpreters were at the fourth level, valued highly for their special skills and long years of experience in the interior. And at the bottom level were the voyageurs, who were hired as contract workers specifically for their skills and strength in paddling.

Although not necessarily employees, First Nations men and women were essential to the NWC. They acted as guides, interpreters and diplomats, provided the posts with food, shared their knowledge about nature and taught the Nor'Westers wilderness survival skills, including how to make birchbark canoes, snowshoes and sleds. According to Professor W.L. Morton, "NWC was the first successful combination of European capital and business enterprise with Indian skills."

Thompson's First Great Rendezvous

Thompson arrived at Grand Portage on July 22, 1797, for his first rendezvous. He had joined the NWC during the company's glory days, when it was making good profit and its operations were running fairly smoothly. An integral part of that operation was the annual meeting between the partners at its inland headquarters, Grand Portage, located on a relatively sheltered bay on the western shores of Lake Superior in what is now northern Minnesota. From the stockaded fort, Thompson would have seen Lake Superior's largest archipelago, Isle Royale, across the lake to the east, with more than 400 islands and many reefs and shoals. In 1803, a new headquarters was built farther north on Lake Superior. First called Fort Kaministiquia, it was later renamed Fort William in honour of NWC partner William McGillivray.

In early May, the Montreal-based partners, their canoes loaded with trade goods, would start their 1,000-mile journey to Grand Portage. Their route would take them up the Ottawa River, down the French River, into Georgian Bay and the North Channel of Lake Huron, to Sault Ste. Marie and across Lake Superior. At about the same time, the wintering partners from the trading posts in the interior would start heading east to Grand Portage with their canoes laden with furs. The northern voyageurs, calling themselves *hommes du nord* or North Men, began arriving in early July. Many dressed in buckskins, they arrived at Fort Charlotte, the depot on Pigeon River, and carried their furs over a difficult nine-mile portage, known as the Great Carrying Place, before arriving at the Grand Portage headquarters. The portage had 16 resting places or *poses*, spaced between 600 to 900 yards apart.

At Grand Portage, the Montreal partners, the wintering partners and leading traders would discuss the business activities of the past year and make plans for the next. It was also the transportation point for exchanging cargoes; trade goods would go back west, and the season's cargo of furs would head east to Montreal. The highlight of the rendezvous, however, was the grand feast and ball.

Thompson was one of over 1,200 men who arrived in 1797 for the rendezvous. He dined in the Great Hall, partook in the sumptuous feast and watched the voyageurs load up the canoes for their return journeys.

In 1797, the official boundary between British and American territory remained to be surveyed, but under the terms of the Jay Treaty in 1794, anything below the 49th parallel would be considered American territory. Any British posts and forts, including those owned by the NWC and HBC, would have to be removed. This was a great concern for the partners, because it meant moving their fur-trading posts, including their headquarters at Grand Portage.

In light of the treaty conditions, the NWC had an important task for its new surveyor. At the annual meeting, Thompson was instructed to make a survey westward along the 49th parallel (considered likely to be designated the future boundary) and chart the positions of all the NWC posts. Thompson noted that he was also directed "to extend my Surveys to the Missisourie River; visit the Villages of the ancient agricultural Natives who dwelt there; enquire for fossil bones of large animals and any monuments if any, that might throw light on the ancient state of the unknown countries I had to travel over and examine."

Thompson had an incredibly difficult task ahead of him—to complete an exploratory survey of the major rivers and lakes covering the uncharted territory that stretched from Lake Superior to Lake Winnipeg. It would take him into the Swan River Valley, south to the Assiniboine and Souris rivers, overland to Mandan villages on the Missouri River, back to the Assiniboine and up the Red River across the headwaters of the Mississippi, and then over the divide to Lake Superior by way of Fond du Lac House (near today's Superior, Wisconsin). He would then have to circumnavigate the world's largest body of fresh water, Lake Superior, and report back to Grand Portage in July 1798.

The Journey Begins

On August 9, 1797, Thompson set out from Grand Portage on one of his most remarkable journeys. It began in the four-canoe northern brigade commanded by Hugh "Laird" McGillis, a former clerk now in charge of the Swan River district. Their route was the "voyageur's highway": Pigeon River, Rainy River, Rainy Lake, Lake of the Woods and then descending the Winnipeg River to Lake Winnipeg. They crossed Lake Winnipeg, paddled the Dauphin River, crossed Lake Manitoba, portaged to Lake Winnipegosis and continued up its west shore.

The canoe brigade separated on September 19, with McGillis going up the Red Deer River and Thompson travelling to Swan River House. After a day's rest, Thompson and Cuthbert Grant, an NWC wintering partner at Assiniboine, rode along the shores of the Swan River. They overnighted at an NWC post on the Snake River before arriving on September 25 at Grant's House (also known as Aspen House or Upper Post) on the Assiniboine.

The Scottish-born Grant had been one of the first NWC traders into Athabasca country. After the 1793 rendezvous at Grand Portage, Grant travelled to the confluence of the

Souris and Assiniboine rivers to establish the first NWC post in the area. Two years after Thompson's visit, Grant died at Grand Portage in 1799. His son, also named Cuthbert, later gained notoriety as one of the Metis leaders in the Battle of Seven Oaks.

Thompson surveyed up the headwaters of the Assiniboine River, as well as the Stone Indian River, noting in October that he had ridden across a mile-long beaver dam with 52 beaver houses. On November 28, Thompson started his journey southwest across the plains to the Mandan villages on the Missouri River. He left McDonnell's House, located at the junction of the Assiniboine and Souris rivers, with nine men, a few horses and 30 dogs and arrived at Old Ash House on the Souris River on December 7. Unable to get a guide, Thompson decided to lead the expedition himself. Travelling by way of Turtle Mountain, the convoy battled severe snowstorms as it crossed the plains, reaching the Missouri River on December 29 and arriving at the first of the five Mandan villages a day later. The 238-mile winter trek had taken 33 days; in good weather, it could have been completed in 10 days.

For years, Europeans had been intrigued about the mysterious Mandan people, who were reported to have light hair and fair complexions. Some believed that the Mandans' ancestors were from Wales, members of a fabled band of Welshmen who reportedly had arrived in North America in 1170 with Prince Madoc. Others theorized the Mandans were descendants of Scandinavians who had travelled to the

At the Mandan village of Mitutanka, Thompson was introduced to the Mandan chief Sheheke, also known as Big White or White Coyote. DON MCMASTER, COURTESY OF RON PENIUK

heart of North America, while some suggested they were one of the Ten Lost Tribes of Israel.

Thompson visited all five of the Mandan agricultural villages, which stretched along the banks of the Missouri River for over 11 miles. The palisaded villages were protected by 10-foot-high stockades with thick posts driven two feet into the ground. Each house in the village was dome-shaped, about 40 feet in diameter and 18 feet high, with a six-foot-long covered porch leading to a door covered by bison skin. Inside, the family lived on the left side, while on the right were stalls for their horses, which were brought in at night. The houses were spaced 15 to 30 feet apart, though not organized in any particular plan. "On looking down on them from the upper bank of the River, they appeared like so many large hives clustered together," wrote Thompson.

He observed, "The dress of the Men is of leather, soft and white. The covering for the body is like a large shirt with sleeves; some wear the Bison leather with the hair on for winter dress, with a leather belt; the leggings [are] of soft white leather, so long as to pass over the belt; their shoes are made of Bison, with the hair on, and always a Bison Robe. The Women's dress is a shirt of Antelope or Deer leather, which ties over the shoulder and comes down to the feet, with a belt round the waist, short leggings to the knee, and Bison Robe shoes . . . They are a handsome people."

At the main Mandan village of Mitutanka (also known as Matooktonka, and, by archaeologists, as Deapolis), Thompson was introduced to the Mandan chief, Sheheke (a name meaning coyote in Mandan), also known as Big White or White Coyote for his light complexion. Thompson told Sheheke that he had not come as a trader, but rather as an NWC representative wanting to see the country and talk to the Mandans about coming north to trade so they could be "more regularly supplied with Arms, Ammunition and other articles they much wanted." The French Canadians with him, however, had sleds full of goods to trade with the Mandans. During his short stay, Thompson developed a 375-word Mandan dictionary.

On January 10, 1798, Thompson left the Mandans. His group now included two Sioux women, former prisoners of the Mandans. But the women weren't on a journey to freedom; rather, they had been bought by the French Canadians, who intended to sell them to other Canadians once they arrived back at the trading house.

Fourteen days later, the entourage reached the Souris River, but it would be another 10 days before they arrived back at McDonnell's House. During their three-week stay there, Thompson wrote his notes and prepared for the journey to the Red and Mississippi rivers and on to Lake Superior.

On February 26, Thompson and his men left the post on foot, walking beside the dog team, and followed an eastward course to the mouth of the Assiniboine River. On March 7, they left the forks of the Assiniboine River (the site of present-day Winnipeg, Manitoba). Travelling on ice, a week later they crossed the 49th parallel and reached the post of Charles Chaboillez on the Pembina River. Thompson wrote, "Our journey for the last eight days has been most wretched travelling; the Snow was full three feet deep; the ice of the River had much water on it, from the mild weather, with small showers of rain, or wet snow."

Tales of Windigo and War

After a week with Chaboillez, they proceeded up the frozen Red River, ascended Red Lake River to the mouth of the Clearwater River and reached the NWC post of Jean-Baptiste Cadotte on March 25. It was here that Thompson waited for the ice to break up, as "snow thawing made the open country like a lake of open water." While at Cadotte's place, Thompson told the fur trader about a Windigo incident that had taken place just a few months earlier on Lake of the Woods. According to Thompson:

> About twenty families were together for hunting and fishing. One morning a young man of about twenty two years of age, on getting up, said he felt a strong inclination to eat his Sister; as he was a steady young man and a promising hunter, no notice was taken of this expression. The next morning he said the same, and repeated the same several times in the day for a few days. His Parents attempted to reason him out of his horrid inclination; he was silent and gave them no answer. His Sister and her Husband became alarmed, left the place, and went to another Camp. He became aware of it; and then said he must have human flesh to eat, and would have it; in other respects his behaviour was cool, calm and quiet. His father and relations were much grieved; argument had no effect on him, and he made them no answer to their questions.

Thompson explained that the father was called to the council, where the state of the young man was discussed and a decision reached that an evil spirit had taken possession and made him a man-eater, a Windigo. The council also found fault with the father for not calling to his assistance a medicine man, who by sweating and his songs to the tambour and rattle might have driven away the evil spirit before it was too late. Thompson continued: "Sentence of death was passed on him, which was to be done by his

Father. The young man was called, and told to sit down in the middle . . . which he did, he was then informed of the resolution taken, to which he said, 'I am willing to die.'" The unhappy father rose and strangled his son. Two hours later, the body was cremated to ashes, "Not the least bit of bone remaining. This was carefully done to prevent his soul and the evil Spirit which possessed him from returning to this world and appearing at his grave, which they believe the souls of those who are buried can and may do, as having a claim to the bones of their bodies."

Thompson added, "It may be thought the Council acted a cruel part in ordering the father to put his Son to death, when they could have ordered it by the hands of another person. This was done to prevent the law of retaliation, which, had it been done by the hands of any other person, might have been a pretext of revenge by those who were not the friends of the person who put him to death."

Speaking of the Windigo, he remarked to Cadotte, "I have known a few instances of this deplorable turn of mind . . . There is yet a dark chapter to be written on this aberration of the human mind."

Thompson finished telling his story just before the Chippewa chief Sheshepaskut arrived with some of his men. The old chief joined the veteran traders, and they talked about the Cheyenne-Chippewa wars that had been going on for years. Thompson asked the chief whether his warriors were involved in the brutal destruction of a Cheyenne village (now known as the Biesterfeldt site in North Dakota). The chief admitted that yes, they had "entered the Village and put every one to death, except three Women; after taking every thing we wanted, we quickly set fire to the Village." Cadotte then finished the story for the chief, telling in gruesome detail of the death of one of the three captive women.

Thompson was surprised that while the Chippewa understood him when he spoke in their language, he had trouble understanding them. They replied, "We understand him because he speaks the language of our Fathers, which we have much changed and made better."

Discovering the Headwaters of the Mississippi

While waiting for the rivers to become clear of ice, Thompson built an 18-by-3-foot birchbark canoe, and on April 19, he left Cadotte's house accompanied by three French Canadians and the Native wife of one of the men. "We set out to survey the country to the source of the Mississippi River," he wrote.

They paddled 64 miles on the fast-moving Clearwater River, headed for Red Lake, where Thompson stopped to visit Chief Sheshepaskut at his camp. The Chippewa asked Thompson if they could use his canoe for some night spearfishing; he agreed, eager to record the activity in his journals. He later wrote:

The spearing of fish in the night is a favorite mode with them, and gives to them a considerable part of their livelihood. The Spear handle is a straight pole of ten to twelve feet in length, headed with a barbed iron. A rude narrow basket of iron hoops is fixed to a pole of about six feet in length. A quantity of birch rind is collected and loosely tied in small parcels. When the night comes, the darker the better, two Men and a Boy embark in a Canoe, the one gently and quietly to give motion to the Canoe. The pole and basket is fixed in the Bow under which the Spearman stands, the Birch Rind is set on fire, and burns with a bright light, but only for a short time [and] the Boy from behind feeds the light so as to keep a constant blaze. The approach of the flaming light seems to stupify the fish, as they are all speared in [a] quiescent state. The Lake or River is thus explored for several hours until the Birch Rind is exhausted.

That night, the Chippewa speared three 60-pound sturgeon, a fish Thompson called "Water Hog."

The next day, Thompson and his group crossed Red Lake, but it was hard going as they were forced to paddle through patches of ice. To keep them moving, Thompson made a "rude Sledge" to carry their canoe and baggage, harnessed himself and the men to the front of it and hauled it more than 15 miles over the ice.

On another part of the journey, they crossed a gigantic swamp, over four miles across. "We passed by means of a few sticks laid lengthways and when we slipped off we sunk to our waists . . . [and] with difficulty regained our footing on the sticks," wrote Thompson, adding, "No woods grow on the great swamp except scattered pine shrubs a few feet in height . . . It is a sad piece of work." It took a day to pass through the strange and eerie landscape.

"Our journey has been very harassing and fatiguing," wrote Thompson, "from Pond to Pond and Brook to Brook with many carrying places, the Ponds or small Lakes were some open, others wholly or partly covered with ice [and] the Brooks so winding, that after paddling an hour we appeared to have made little or no advance."

On April 27, 19 days after leaving Cadotte's post, Thompson arrived at Turtle Lake (near present-day Bemidji, Minnesota). He believed he had discovered the legendary source of the mighty Mississippi. Later, during his lifetime, it was determined that nearby Lake Itasca was the actual source; however, since Turtle Lake was the most northerly part of the river, many still credit Thompson with the discovery.

Years later, Thompson referred to the Mississippi River as "the most magnificent River . . . of North America" and compared it to the Nile River in Africa:

To the intelligent part of mankind, the sources of all the great rivers have always been subjects of curiosity; witness the expeditions undertaken, the sums of money expended, and the sufferings endured to discover the sources of the Nile, the research of ages. Whatever the Nile had been in ancient times in Art and Arms, the noble valley of the Mississippi bids fair to be, and excluding its pompous, useless Pyramids and other works, its anglo saxon population will fair exceed the Egyptians in all the arts of civilized life and in a pure religion. Although these are the predictions of a solitary traveller unknown to the world they will surely be verified.

The source of the Nile was not identified until 1862, five years after Thompson's death.

By the time Thompson reached Cass Lake, his canoe had sprung a leak. Luckily, two canoes of Chippewayans came by and took him to the lake's trading post, Red Cedar Lake House, managed by John Sayer, an NWC wintering partner. According to Thompson, Sayer and his men had survived the winter on wild rice and maple sugar that had been made in the spring by both the Natives and Canadian fur traders. Thompson thought the maple sugar as good as the sugars from the West Indies.

After Sayer gave them a new canoe, Thompson's group left Cass Lake on May 3 and seven days later arrived at Fond du Lac House, at the southwestern end of Lake Superior. At one point of the journey, after commenting that without the "crookedness" of the Mississippi River, the current would be too strong for any boat to ascend, Thompson reflected, "I have always admired the formations of the Rivers, as directed by the finger of God for the most benevolent purposes."

Journey's End

On May 12, 1798, Thompson began his survey of Lake Superior, paddling in a counter-clockwise direction, starting at its westernmost point, near today's Duluth, Minnesota, and Superior, Wisconsin. Sixteen days later, he reached Sault Ste. Marie at the eastern end of the lake.

It had been a harrowing journey on Lake Superior, an unpredictable and dangerous lake where terrible storms rise without notice. Near Michigan's Keweenaw Peninsula, Thompson had feared the strong waves would push lake ice closer to shore, smashing their canoes against the steep rocks. On another day, they were caught on the lake during a heavy rainstorm, with "vivid Lightning and loud Thunder."

Along with the hazards faced on the lake, food provisions were meagre. They lived on hulled corn, a partial bag of wild rice and a few pounds of grease to assist in boiling. "It is customary after supper to boil Corn or rice for the meals of the next day, and in good weather we set off by 4 AM. The Kettles were taken off the fire in a boiling state and placed in the Canoe, and two hours after we had a warm breakfast," wrote Thompson.

When Thompson reached Sault Ste. Marie on May 28, 1798, he briefly met with Alexander Mackenzie, the celebrated explorer who had made the famous journey of discovery to the Pacific Ocean in 1793, and for whom the powerful Mackenzie River was named. Mackenzie praised the 28-year-old Thompson, telling him that what he had accomplished in 10 months Mackenzie would have expected to take two years to achieve.

One June 1, Thompson left Sault Ste. Marie in a canoe

with some of the NWC's most powerful individuals, including William McGillivray and Mackenzie. Six days later, they arrived at Grand Portage. Since the last rendezvous, Thompson had travelled and surveyed almost 4,000 miles of the wildest interior of North America and completed the first formal mapping of the future states of Minnesota and North Dakota.

The Western Years: 1798–1810

THOMPSON SPENT FIVE WEEKS AT Grand Portage, where he observed both the land and the men. He made a detailed survey of the nine-mile portage between Pigeon River and Grand Portage and witnessed the arrival from Sault Ste. Marie of the company's ship *Otter*, as well as the brigades of the Montreal canoes. He measured Mount Josephine and noted the arrival from the interior of Duncan McGillivray, who was in a stretcher due to a leg injury.

On July 14, 1798, Thompson began his journey back west with a new assignment: to establish a fur-trading post on Lac La Biche (also known as Red Deers Lake) in Athabasca country. The new post, Red Deers Lake House, would be strategically important because Portage La Biche connected

Lac La Biche in the Athabasca and Mackenzie Basin (Pacific watershed) with the Churchill River Basin (Hudson Bay watershed). Thompson was the first to document the existence of Portage La Biche, which would become a critical link in the NWC's trade route to the southern portion of Athabasca country and the Pacific. The following year, the HBC sent their surveyor-trader Peter Fidler to Lac La Biche to build the HBC's first post in Athabasca country, Greenwich House, located right beside the NWC's post, though Thompson had already left by then.

On his way to Lac La Biche, Thompson stopped for the day at Île-à-la-Crosse, the NWC's remote post near the headwaters of the Churchill River, where he met Charlotte, daughter of the post's former manager Patrick Small (one of the original Scottish partners of the NWC) and a Cree woman. Small had married the woman "in the style of the country," and together they had three children: Nancy, Patrick Jr. and Charlotte. When Small sold his NWC shares, he retired from the fur trade and moved to London, England, abandoning his Cree wife and their three children.

Thompson and his three-canoe brigade reached Lac La Biche in early October and built Red Deers Lake House. By late March 1799, Thompson was off again, exploring and surveying the country as far as the mouth of the Clearwater River (the present-day site of Fort McMurray, Alberta). On May 20, on his way to Grand Portage, he stopped at Île-à-la-Crosse and married Charlotte in the "custom of the Cree," which Thompson explained to mean, "The marriages are without noise or ceremony; nothing is requisite but the consent of the parties and the parents . . . when contrariety of disposition prevails, so that they cannot live peaceably together, they separate with as little ceremony as they came together, and both parties are free to attach themselves to whom they will, without any stain on their characters." At the time of their marriage, Thompson was 29 and Charlotte only 13 years old, but their union of almost 58 years became one of Canada's greatest love stories.

Accompanied by Charlotte, Thompson continued on to Grand Portage for the annual meeting and rendezvous. Later, they wintered on the North Saskatchewan River at Fort George, near the HBC's Buckingham House. Fort George, a stockaded group of shanties, was built in 1792; three years later, it was a busy place with 110 men (the rival HBC had only 35). However, when the Thompsons arrived in 1799, they found the post in a dilapidated condition. It was abandoned a year after they left.

Crossing the Rockies

In the spring of 1800, Thompson rode to Rocky Mountain House, the new post at the headwaters of the North Saskatchewan River. It was the NWC's most westerly post, built the year before by his brother-in-law, John McDonald of Garth, who had married Charlotte's sister, Nancy. Thompson did some surveying in the area before returning to Fort George on May 12. Six days later, the Thompsons left for Grand Portage and, after the annual meeting, travelled to Rocky Mountain House, his new posting.

The NWC had ordered Thompson and the post's manager, Duncan McGillivray, to find a practical route over the Rockies and to start trade with the First Nations people on the other side. Three weeks after arriving at Rocky Mountain House, Thompson rode to meet a party of Kutenai who were coming over the mountains to trade. Nine days later, accompanied by five Nor'Westers, as well as his Peigan guide, Old Bear, and a Cree named He Dog, Thompson reached the Kutenai group of 26 men and 7 women.

The historic trading breakthrough, however, was marred by danger and tension. To get to Rocky Mountain House, the Kutenai had to pass through the foothills territory of their Peigan enemies, who opposed the idea of the Kutenai doing business with any white trader. Throughout the trek to the post, a large group of Peigan warriors shadowed and harassed the convoy, trying to stop them. The warriors stole some of the group's horses, including Thompson's, challenged the Kutenai, blocked their path and tried to force them back over the mountains. But with determination, bravery and Thompson's encouragement, the Kutenai resisted and continued on. In his October 16 journal entry, Thompson wrote:

> I cannot help admiring the Spirit of these brave, undaunted, but poor Kootenaes. They have all along shown a courage and

Fortitude admirable—not the least sign of Weakness or Cow-
ardice—altho' they are in the Power of a large Party of Indians,
who are at least 20 to one. They [the Kutenai] are conducted
by 4 old Men who seem worthy of being at the Head of such
People. This day when the younger Pekenow [Peigan] Men
seized the Heads of their Horses, they all as if acted by one
Soul bent their Bows, got ready their Weapons, and prepared
to make their Oppressors quit their Horses or sell their Lives
dearly—hardly a single Word was spoken among them.

In spite of the aggressive actions of the Peigan, the group
arrived at Rocky Mountain House on October 20. The
Kutenai traded their furs and left two days later, accompanied by two French Canadians sent by Thompson to winter
with them. The Kutenai promised to return the following
summer, as well as send a guide in the spring to lead an
NWC expedition over the mountains.

About a month later, on November 17, Thompson
rode down to the Bow Valley, accompanied by Duncan
McGillivray, who was in charge of Rocky Mountain House,
and four others. Along the route, Thompson surveyed the
rivers and creeks and stopped to visit a Peigan camp. Almost
20 years before, Thompson had wintered by the Bow River
with the Peigan, learning much about their culture and tra-
ditions. Now, however, he knew that the Peigan opposed
the idea of white traders crossing the Rockies to trade with
their enemies, the Kutenai. The men arrived back at Rocky
Mountain House on December 3.

During the winter months of 1800–1801, Thompson and McGillivray planned their spring expedition across the Rockies, optimistic of success but aware of the Peigan's animosity toward their plans. However, things started to go wrong once spring arrived. First, the guide sent by the Kutenai to lead them across the mountains was murdered a few miles from Rocky Mountain House. Then McGillivray became ill with rheumatism and had to be replaced as expedition leader by senior trader James Hughes. (Hughes' daughter was married to Charlotte's brother, Patrick Small Jr.)

The expedition needed an experienced First Nations guide; however, the choices were limited. McGillivray hired a Cree known as The Rook, who had bragged that he had previously crossed the mountains on a good horse trail. Thompson and others doubted the Cree's claim from the beginning, but nevertheless, the 14-member expedition, including The Rook, his wife and another woman, left Rocky Mountain House on horseback on June 7, 1801. Hughes was in command with Thompson as his second. They headed west on the North Saskatchewan River for 22 miles, and then The Rook led them up the North Ram River.

The expedition continued to be jinxed. They battled heavy rain, steep climbs, rough terrain, small bogs and floods. The North Ram River was swollen with spring run-off, making it extremely difficult for the horse brigade to travel. Then, on Saturday, June 13, The Rook led them to an impassable spot: a deep lake surrounded by high cliffs. After

Ram River Falls is one of the numerous obstacles that blocked Thompson's 1800 attempt to cross the Rocky Mountains.

GLENBOW ARCHIVES NA-4093-60

being questioned by Hughes and Thompson, he admitted that he had lied about crossing the mountains with horses. "We had no Horses with us—we left them with our Families, at the Entrance into the Mountains," he told them. "But I thought where we had gone on Foot, Horses might possibly go—but I forgot this Part of the Mountain."

Unable to find an alternative route for the horses, Hughes halted the expedition. However, while Hughes took the horses and some of the people back to Rocky Mountain House, Thompson and eight voyageurs built a canoe and paddled up the North Saskatchewan River. But the spring run-off made the river dangerous and torrential with currents racing at 12 to 15 miles per hour. After three days, they turned the canoe around and let the current take them down to Rocky Mountain House, arriving back on June 30. During Thompson's absence, Charlotte had given birth to their first child, a daughter named Fanny, born on June 10, 1801, at Rocky Mountain House.

Determined to cross the Rockies the following year, Thompson wrote letters to Duncan McGillivray and McGillivray's brother William, explaining the expedition's failure and his plans to successfully cross the mountains the following year. To indulge his passion for mapmaking, Thompson took a survey trip on horseback to Fort Augustus (the site of present-day Edmonton) before winter set in.

However, NWC priorities were changing. The company's long-time plans to expand westward to the Pacific were set aside, and it focused on meeting the challenge to its trading operations in the fur-rich regions of northern Alberta, Saskatchewan and Manitoba. Before Thompson could launch his 1802 expedition to cross the mountains, he was assigned for the next four years to trading posts east of the Rockies, starting in Peace River country.

Back to Muskrat Country

After spending the winter of 1801–2 at Rocky Mountain House, Thompson and his family left in May and attended the 1802 rendezvous at Grand Portage, the last one at that location. Then the Thompson family headed north to Peace River Forks (also called Forks of the Peace and Fort Fork), the site of present-day Peace River, Alberta, arriving in the cold month of November. Before the year ended, Thompson had surveyed the ancient Cree Kinistineuu War Trail to Peace River from today's Grouard, Alberta. According to the journals of Alexander Mackenzie, the trail had been used until about 1782 by the Cree to make war on northern tribes.

Thompson spent most of 1803 at Peace River Forks, trading, keeping the post's journal and recording activities. On June 5, he noted that their competitor, XY Company, was building a post barely 100 yards away. Thompson also kept a meteorological journal and carried out some surveying excursions, including a two-week dogsled trip in mid-December to Lesser Slave Lake.

On March 5, 1804, at Peace River Forks, the Thompsons' second child, Samuel, was born. Ten days later, Thompson, Charlotte and their two children began their long journey to Fort Kaministiquia, the NWC's new headquarters on Lake Superior (later renamed Fort William). They travelled on ice 18 miles down the Peace River to Horse Shoe House, at the mouth of the Notikewin River, where they waited for the river ice to clear. On May 12, the family arrived at Fort Chipewyan, and five days later reached the mouth of the Clearwater River before heading to Lake Superior.

At the NWC council meeting, Thompson received a prestigious promotion to wintering partner and was assigned back to the familiar Athabasca territory he called Muskrat

Country. On his return west, Thompson journeyed on the old "voyageur's trail" recently rediscovered by Nor'Wester Roderick Mackenzie. It was an ancient Aboriginal water highway to the west that passed entirely through British territory. The brigade went up the Kaministiquia River, across Dog Lake, up Dog River, across to Lac des Mille Lacs, then to Lac La Croix and Rainy Lake before merging with the existing NWC route to the west. Thompson left his men at Cranberry Lake to build a post while he continued down the Churchill River, arriving at Musquawegan (Bear's Backbone) Post on October 6, where he wintered and competed for furs against his old schoolmate, the HBC's George Charles.

On May 27 to 28, 1805, Thompson travelled to the most northeasterly point of his NWC career—about 250 miles from Churchill Factory on Hudson Bay, where he had first worked when he arrived in 1784. When he returned to Cranberry Lake on June 27, he heard the good news that there was one less fur-trade rival to contend with: the NWC and XY Company had merged on November 5, 1804.

About a month later, Thompson left for his old trading grounds on Reindeer Lake, arriving August 4. Leaving Benjamin Frobisher to build a post, Thompson went on to build a house and winter at Reed Lake, where he had stayed 11 years before while working for the HBC. The Thompsons' third child, Emma, was born at Reed Lake House in March 1806. When Thompson and his family left Muskrat Country on June 10, 1806, he had completed his survey and astronomical observations for the area. He never returned there again.

Thompson headed to Lake Superior for the 1806 annual meeting at Fort William, where he was ordered to return to Rocky Mountain House on the North Saskatchewan River to find a practical route across the Rockies and establish trade relations on the western side. The Thompson family arrived at Rocky Mountain House on September 11.

The Peigan were still against white traders going across the mountains to trade guns to the Kutenai. The Peigan chief Kootanee Apee visited Thompson at Rocky Mountain House on January 1 and again in March. Did Thompson's old friend warn him of violence if he continued with his plan to cross the Rockies and set up trade on the other side? Or did the two men come to a workable agreement? There is no record of their conversation, so no one knows.

On May 10, 1807, Thompson left Rocky Mountain House to embark on his expedition across the mountains, accompanied by Charlotte, their three young children and seven French Canadians. By coincidence or luck, the Peigan warriors who had threatened to stop Thompson from crossing the mountains had taken their war party to Montana to avenge the death of two warriors, giving Thompson the opportunity to cross the Rockies in safety.

By June 25, the convoy had reached the height of land that Thompson later named Howse Pass, after HBC trader Joseph Howse. The ascent to the pass had been easy, but the descent down the steep western slope was challenging, especially when crossing the raging Blaeberry River. "The Horses with difficulty crossed and recrossed at every 2 or 300 yards, & the Men crossed by clinging to the Tails & Manes of the Horses, & yet ran no small Danger of being swept away & drowned," wrote Thompson. After June 30, they camped near the mouth of the Blaeberry for several days, building canoes and repacking. The canoe brigade reached Lake Windermere in mid-July and started building Kootenae House on the lake's west side. Thompson and his family remained at Kootenae House for the rest of the year, where he traded with the Native people, measured mountains and made his astronomical observations.

While Thompson makes no mention of it in his journals or *Narrative*, during his stay at Kootenae House, he seems to acknowledge he fathered a son and abandoned the child and mother when he was in Athabasca country, presumably before he married Charlotte. In a letter to Donald McTavish, an NWC agent and partner in the Athabasca region, Thompson wrote, "I must now again beg of you to take my little child under your protection and if possible to get him from his mother . . . you might send him to Fort Augustus or contrive some way or other to put him in my hands . . . at least see him well-clothed and of course charge it to my account." To date, the child remains unidentified, adding another mystery to the life of Thompson.

On April 20, 1808, Thompson descended the Kootenay

River. A week later, he reached Tobacco River, Montana, and eight days later, the camp of the Flatheads and Kutenai near today's Bonner's Ferry in Idaho. He was back at Kootenay House on June 8.

Taking his family with him, Thompson then went north, crossing the mountains with furs obtained during the year and reaching Kootenay Plains on June 22. Along the way, the group killed and ate several of their horses for food. At Kootenay Plains, they embarked on a canoe, descended the North Saskatchewan River and stopped at Boggy Hall (near the present-day site of Drayton Valley, Alberta). Thompson left his family at Boggy Hall, where Charlotte's brother, Patrick Small, was posted, and continued on to Rainy Lake House, arriving on August 2. Rainy Lake House was now the turnaround depot for brigades from Athabasca country and the Columbia region, as it was too far to go to Fort William and back before winter set in.

Two days later, Thompson began his return journey. On August 18, while on the western shore of Lake Winnipeg, he was joined by Alexander Henry, who was on his way to Fort Vermilion. While on the lake, they may have witnessed NWC brigades racing each other.

The North Men were a daring group of voyageurs who liked adventure and taking risks, especially on Lake Winnipeg, their favourite body of water for racing. The brigades would challenge each other to race, drop their sails and line up to start amid loud cheering. Duncan McGillivray's journal recorded one epic race between Athabasca (considered the best racers) and another northern brigade that continued non-stop for two days and nights. The race ended in a draw when the exhausted crews, "being entirely overcome with labour and fatigue, agreed to camp and cross the rest of the Lake together," according to McGillivray.

About a month later, Thompson reached Fort Vermilion and then rode to Boggy Hall, leaving his canoe brigade to paddle up the North Saskatchewan River. Thompson's fourth child, John Thompson, had been born at Boggy Hall on August 25, 1808. Thompson arrived there on October 3 and later continued on horseback to Kootenae House, arriving on November 2 to spend the winter. (Charlotte and the children wintered at Fort Augustus.)

The next year, Thompson left Kootenae House on April 17 and two months later was back at Fort Augustus visiting for a few weeks with Charlotte and his children, as well as with his old friend James Hughes. He headed back west across the mountains on horseback on July 18. Before crossing Howse Pass, Thompson had breakfast with the HBC's Joseph Howse near the Kootenay Plains on August 9. Howse was returning from a scouting trip to the mountains in preparation for crossing the Rockies the following year. The two men may well have known each other from Thompson's time with the HBC, as Howse had arrived at York Factory from England in 1795 to be the post's writer. In 1810, Howse became the first HBC trader to cross the Rockies.

By September 10, 1809, Thompson was south again, this time on the eastern shore of Pend d'Oreille Lake, where he and his men built Kullyspell House. A few weeks later, he set off on horseback to survey the area, returning to the post on October 6 and then meeting his canoe brigade of trade goods at the Kootenay River. Sending his horse ahead, he paddled with James McMillan back to Kullyspell House, arriving on October 30. Thompson soon left again, on horseback, to build Saleesh House (near present-day Thompson Falls, Montana), where he spent the winter of 1809–10.

Author Jack Nisbet tells of another mystery in Thompson's life. He writes, "Although most historians write about Thompson's lifelong faithfulness to Charlotte, rumours about his time at Saleesh House have circulated among the local people." Apparently, a man from the area told a newspaper reporter that "David Thompson was a great man. He lived among my people . . . He had a woman among the Salish. His descendants still live on the reservation." Nisbet adds the man's sister told an interviewer "that Thompson had a daughter by a Pend Oreille woman."

During the winter he spent at Saleesh House, Thompson continued to take astronomical observations, lugging his telescope to a plateau several hundred feet above the post. The Salish, who usually had some members accompany him, gave Thompson the name Koo Koo Sint, the Man Who Looks at Stars.

7

The Race for the Columbia: 1810–1812

THOMPSON WAS LOOKING FORWARD TO 1810. Once he had brought the furs to Fort William, he was heading to Montreal to begin a 10-month furlough. It would be the first time in 26 years that he would be out of the wilderness. On May 9, he headed over the mountains, leaving his long-time assistant, Finan McDonald, to operate Saleesh House, James McMillan at Kullyspell (after he brought the furs east), and sending Jacques Raphael (Jaco) Finley to build Spokane House (near present-day Spokane, Washington). The three posts gave the Salish, allies of the Kutenai, direct access to guns and iron, which further angered their Peigan enemies.

When Thompson stopped at Rocky Mountain House on his way east, he heard that the Peigan had threatened violent death to white traders who attempted to cross the mountains. A similar warning had been given to Joseph Howse when he led the HBC expedition over the mountains in 1810, as noted by the HBC's James Bird in his journal entry of May 13, 1811: "The Muddy River Indians [Peigan] have promised not to molest Mr. Howse . . . but declared that, if they ever again met with a white Man going to supply their Enemies, they would not only plunder & kill him, but that they would make dry Meat of his body. This threat they are sufficiently brutal to fulfill to its utmost extent."

The Battle with the Peigan

While Thompson was paddling toward Rainy Lake House in July, back in Montana, Finan McDonald had gone buffalo hunting with the Salish. McDonald and Nor'Westers Baptiste Buché and Michel Bourdeaux had accompanied a party of 150 Salish hunters over the mountains east of Saleesh (Flathead) Lake into the eastern plains country of the Peigan. The Salish no longer feared the Peigan, as they had traded furs for firearms and iron arrowheads from Thompson's post the previous winter.

McDonald and his party were camped close to the hunting grounds when the Salish scouts rushed into camp one morning, yelling, "The enemy is on us." Quickly, the tents were toppled and baggage piled on top to form a barrier. Soon, about 170 Peigan warriors on horseback charged the Salish, trying to break the hastily built defensive rampart.

When they couldn't break the line, the Peigan warriors dismounted about 400 yards away and an all-day battle with guns, bows and arrows, and lances began.

By evening, 7 Peigan were dead and 13 wounded, and the Salish lost 5 men, with 9 injured. McDonald had fired 45 shots at the Peigan, killing 2 and injuring 1; both French Canadians had fired 43 times, each wounding 1 Peigan.

The defeated Peigan were furious at the white traders for providing arms to the Salish and fighting alongside them. The Peigan now considered all white traders to be enemies and vowed to stop access over the mountains, the NWC's vital trade route to the west.

Back to the Columbia

Meanwhile, Thompson had reached Rainy Lake House on July 22, 1810. Waiting for him was an order he had not expected: he was directed to immediately return west, cross the Rockies and establish a trading post at the mouth of the Columbia River before the Americans did.

Why the sudden panic to get Thompson to the river's mouth? The NWC had heard that American fur trader John Jacob Astor was sending two expeditions—one by sea and one by land—to claim the river's mouth for his expanding fur-trade empire.

Astor was a German immigrant, born in 1763, who had come to America when he was 20 years old. He chose a career in the fur trade and by 1800 was a successful and wealthy financier, sending his best furs to China and bringing back exotic goods to sell in the US and Europe. Astor envisioned an empire stretching from the Missouri River to the lower Columbia River, competing with the HBC and NWC. His plan was to have his furs shipped west to the Columbia and from there to China, whereas both the NWC and HBC shipped their furs east to Montreal and Hudson Bay respectively and then across the Atlantic Ocean to markets in Europe.

According to historian Jean Morrison, the race for the Columbia Basin caught the attention of President Thomas Jefferson, who interpreted a passage from Alexander Mackenzie's book *Voyages from Montreal* as a "threat to the territorial ambitions of the United States." The passage read: "Whatever course may be taken from the Atlantic, the Columbia is the line of communication from the Pacific Ocean, pointed out by nature . . . By opening this intercourse between the Atlantic and Pacific Oceans . . . the entire command of the fur trade might be obtained."

The American historian Stephen E. Ambrose writes, "The news that the British were threatening to set up shop in the Northwest galvanized Jefferson into manic activity." In 1803, Jefferson accepted France's offer to sell Louisiana to the US for $15 million, a deal that doubled the size of America. The new lands stretched from the Mississippi River to the Rockies and from the Gulf of Mexico to about the 49th parallel, an area larger than Great Britain, France, Germany, Italy, Spain and Portugal combined.

The Rocky Mountains now formed the western boundary of the US. A year later, Jefferson commissioned his secretary, Meriwether Lewis, and mapmaker William Clark to explore this newest piece of American real estate and beyond it to the Pacific Ocean. He knew the British fur traders controlled the fur trade west of the Mississippi and north into Canada, and his goal was to "expand the United States and wrest the fur trade from the British." (The expedition used Thompson's map of the upper Missouri in preparing for the expedition and carried a tracing of his map on their journey; a notation written by Jefferson on the map credits Thompson.)

Jean Morrison writes, "After their two-year journey, the explorers urged the United States government to forestall North West Company ambitions on the Pacific by the 'establishment of a trading post at the mouth of the Columbia River, for expediting the commerce of furs to China.' These proposals reinforced similar plans already forming in the mind of John Jacob Astor."

In 1803, when the US purchased Louisiana (the drainage basin of the Mississippi River), it legally closed the door on Canadian traders but opened up new expansion opportunities for American traders. In 1808, Astor organized the American Fur Company and offered the NWC the option to buy a one-third interest in his new Pacific Coast venture. The Montreal-based NWC agents had reservations about

In 1803, after Grand Portage was abandoned by the NWC because it was in American territory, Fort William, on the western shores of Lake Superior, became the new NWC headquarters and site of the annual meeting and rendezvous. FORT WILLIAM HISTORICAL PARK

the deal and brought it for discussion with the wintering partners at the 1810 rendezvous at Fort William.

Jean Morrison states that the wintering partners were considering accepting Astor's offer until Simon McGillivray spoke against it: "If you do not oppose the Americans beyond the Mountains they will bye and bye meet you on this side; and even if you should ultimately be inclined to make an amicable arrangement with them, the only way to do so upon an independent footing, or to obtain good terms, is to have rival establishments previously formed in the Country on the same footing as theirs." Gaining that footing now became crucial to the NWC. The partners wanted Thompson to immediately set forth to travel the Columbia River to the Pacific and establish a trading post at its mouth.

The council ended on July 18. By the time Thompson arrived at Rainy Lake four days later, his new orders were waiting for him. A few days later, he headed back west with 6 canoes, 24 men and more than 6,000 tons of trade goods. While somewhat disappointed about his cancelled furlough, Thompson saw an opportunity that had eluded him before—the chance to complete his survey of the Columbia River and create his dream: a detailed map from Hudson Bay to Lake Superior to the Pacific.

By the time Thompson was on his way, Astor had formed the Pacific Fur Company, a subsidiary of the American Fur Company. Astor's land crew began their race to the mouth of the Columbia River from St. Louis, Missouri, in early July; the steamer *Tonquin* left from New York on September 11, headed for the same destination. The race between the NWC and the Pacific Fur Company to claim the Pacific watershed was now on, and whoever reached the mouth of the Columbia first would be the winner.

A Peigan Blockade

On his voyage back west, Thompson and his Columbia brigade brought his family to winter at Fort Augustus. Here,

Charlotte would give birth to their fifth child, Joshua, on March 28, 1811.

The Columbia brigade separated into two groups at Fort Vermilion on the North Saskatchewan River, one group travelling on land and the other on water, with plans to meet every three days. Thompson, along with William Henry (Alexander Henry's cousin) and two Iroquois hunters, went ahead on horseback, hunting and providing game for the canoe brigade. Thompson intended the two parties to merge into one canoe brigade at Rocky Mountain House and continue up the river to Kootenay Plains, where a voyageur, Bercier, would be waiting with horses to carry the cargo over the Rockies through Howse Pass.

The canoe brigade reached Rocky Mountain House first, arriving on September 24, 1810. When they did not see Thompson, they paddled for about a day up the North Saskatchewan River until stopped by a Peigan blockade. Chief Black Bear told them they were not allowed through to cross the mountains; the trade route was shut down by the Peigan. The brigade returned to Rocky Mountain House, where the Peigan continued to watch their movements.

Concern was mounting as to Thompson's whereabouts. He had not been seen nor heard from since the last contact with the brigade on September 15. What had happened to him?

It was later learned that around September 24, Thompson had sent Henry ahead to scout past Rocky Mountain House looking for the canoe brigade. Henry had seen that the Peigan were blocking the river to prevent the brigade from crossing the mountains. Although Thompson did not know about the Peigan defeat by the Salish, he sensed that something serious had happened to provoke them. When one of Thompson's men had fired a shot as a signal to find the canoe brigade, Thompson knew they could now be in danger. "I told them they acted very foolishly, that the Peigans would be on us very early in the morning, and that we must start at the dawn of day and ride for our lives; on this, we acted the next morning and rode off," he later wrote. The Peigan followed the tracks of Thompson's horses, but stopped the chase when they came upon three grizzly bears. Thompson and his men rode until dark and then hid in the woods.

It wasn't until a month later, on October 12, that William Henry brought word to his cousin Alexander, who had stopped at Rocky Mountain House, that Thompson was hiding at a location about 50 to 60 miles downstream. The next day, Alexander and William Henry paddled out to find Thompson. Alexander Henry wrote in his journal, "At noon we embarked and at 4 p.m. reached Thompson's camp, on the N. Side, on top of a hill 300 feet above the water, where tall pines stood so thickly that I could not see his tent until I came within 10 yards of it. He was starving and waiting for his people."

There is still controversy about what really happened during Thompson's four-week absence. The journal entries between July 22, when he left Rainy Lake, and October 29 have disappeared, leaving historians to wonder if Thompson himself, for some reason, threw out his notes. His October 29 posting mentions no details of dates or times, unusual for an experienced record-keeper like Thompson:

> I had often requested permission to change the route across the Mountains, as we must sooner or later be cut off by the Peagan Indians, but the great Partners assured me there was no danger. But this year when near the Mountains . . . I left the Canoes for a day or two to get Provisions . . . Finding the Canoes did not come I sent Mr. Wm Henry and an Indian to learn the cause, and to beware of the Enemies. They returned at night having seen a strong camp of Peagan which [had] driven the Canoes down . . . at dawn of day we had to ride for our lives; they followed us most of the day, but Snow coming on covered our tracks. I had now to find the Canoes and men, and with Horses cross to the Athabaska River.

Thompson decided on an alternative route over the Rockies, one that was out of range of the Peigan. His new plan was to travel along the Stone Trail, an old Assiniboine footpath, still used by Natives, that went west from the North Saskatchewan River. From the trail, he would lead his men up the Athabasca River, over the Rockies by way of Athabasca Pass and to the Columbia River.

He ordered the Columbia brigade to join him downstream. After regrouping on the banks of the North

Saskatchewan River, the group left with 24 men plus 3 of their wives and 24 pack horses loaded with 6,000 pounds of trade goods. A month later, they crossed the Athabasca River, continued to Brûlé Lake and then moved northward five miles, where they stopped and camped for the next four weeks (in an area that is now part of Jasper National Park). During that time, they built sleds and snowshoes for the journey across the mountains.

It was now almost Christmas. The temperatures were cold, and the spirits of the men were low. On December 21, 40-year-old Thompson wrote to his friend Alexander Fraser. The former trader was now retired and living in Montreal. Thompson lamented, "I am getting tired of such constant hard journeys; for the last 20 months I have spent only barely two months under the shelter of a hut, all the rest has been in my tent, and there is little likelihood the next 12 months will be much otherwise."

On December 28, Thompson and 12 men (the others had returned to Rocky Mountain House) loaded up 8 dogsleds and 4 pack horses with their provisions of 280 pounds of pemmican, 35 pounds of grease, 60 pounds of flour, 80 pounds of partly dried meat and some fresh meat. The next day, they set out to cross the Rockies with Thomas, an Iroquois, leading the snowshoe brigade, followed by Thompson and the French Canadians with the sleds and horses.

On January 6, 1811, as they began the difficult ascent to

the pass, the four horses were abandoned at the mouth of the Miette River, and everything was hauled by dogsleds. A day later, in the vicinity of present-day Jasper, Thompson and his men came upon strange tracks, similar to those of the mythical beast now called the Sasquatch. Over the years, Thompson had heard stories from various First Nations about enormous creatures living in woods, but he had discounted them as "Nurse Fables." Now he wasn't sure what to think. He noted the incident in his journal entry for January 7, 1811, and then expanded upon it in his *Narrative*:

> When proceeding up the Athabaska River to cross the Mountains . . . on one of the channels of the River we came to the track of a large animal, which measured fourteen inches in length by eight inches in breadth by a tape line. As the snow was about six inches in depth the track was well defined, and we could see it for a full one hundred yards from us . . . proceeding from north to south. We did not attempt to follow it, we had no time for it, and the Hunters, eager as they are to follow and shoot every animal, made no attempt to follow this beast, for what could the balls of our fowling guns do against such an animal. [A] report from old times had made the head branches of this River and the Mountains in the vicinity the abode of one, or more, very large animals, to which I never appeared to give credence, for these reports appeared to arise from the fondness for the marvelous so common to mankind: but the sight of the track of that large beast staggered me, and I often thought of it, yet never could bring myself to believe such an animal existed.

On January 10, the men reached Athabasca Pass, located at the headwaters of the Whirlpool River (in present-day Jasper National Park). "The view before us was . . . to me a most exhilarating sight . . . My men were not at their ease, yet when night came they admired the brilliancy of the Stars, and as one of them said, he thought he could almost touch them with his hand," wrote Thompson.

As he looked around at the scale of the grandeur, the scientist in him pondered, "One is tempted to enquire what may be the volume of water contained in the immense quantities of snow brought to, and lodged on, the Mountains from the Pacific ocean, and how from an Ocean of salt water the immense evaporation constantly going on is pure fresh water; these are mysterious operations on a scale so vast that the human mind is lost in the contemplation."

The brigade began their descent through deep, wet snow. Seven days later, they reached the Columbia River and hauled sleds for 12 miles before his men mutinied, refusing to go any farther because of the brutal conditions. Thompson was forced to halt the expedition and retreated back to a spot that later became known as the Boat Encampment, where he expected to winter. Throughout the journey, Thompson had lost men either through desertion or when they were sent back to Rocky Mountain House. When he camped on January 26, he had only two men left with him, although a few more returned in February. Over the next few months, Thompson and his men built a canoe, using cedar for the first time rather than birchbark. With ingenuity, they cut the cedar planks with an axe, bent the boards into a canoe frame and sewed them into place with roots from pine trees.

On April 16, their cedar-plank canoe was finished and, according to Thompson, "all ready for our voyage." They were at the Big Bend of the Columbia River (which Thompson called the Kootenay because, at the time, he thought it was a separate river), but didn't know which way to go: south, paddling downstream on the river, or north, paddling upstream?

Thompson chose to go upstream, which took him on a lengthy detour, travelling away from the mouth of the Columbia. If he had paddled downstream, his journey would have taken him across the 180-degree river bend and then on a straight run to the Pacific Ocean. Instead, because of the detour, it took Thompson an extra two months.

Thompson later explained that his decision took into consideration that he had only a small party with him when he set out on April 17, a small party that he judged "too weak to make our way through the numerous Indians we had to pass; so few men would be a temptation to some of them to take what little we had . . . I had to proceed up the River and to the Saleesh country to where I knew I could find the free Hunters and engage some of them to accompany me."

The group reached Lake Windermere on May 14 and

descended the Kootenay River. Travelling by canoe and on horseback and staying at NWC posts along the way, they proceeded to Saleesh House in Montana and eventually Spokane House. Three days of riding brought them to Kettle Falls on the Columbia River, where they built another cedar canoe. On July 3, they paddled down the Columbia, arriving at the mouth of the river on July 15, 1811.

But they were too late. Astor's men had arrived by ship a couple of weeks earlier and had already built their trading post, Fort Astoria. Interestingly, Astor's post was staffed largely by former Nor'Westers, including French-Canadian Gabriel Franchère, who wrote about Thompson's arrival in his journal:

> We saw a large canoe with a flag displayed at her stern rounding the point which we called Tongue Point. We knew not who it could be. We were soon relieved of our uncertainty by the arrival of the canoe, which touched shore at a little wharf that we had built to facilitate the landing of goods. The flag she bore was British, and her crew was composed of eight Canadian boatmen, or voyageurs. A well-dressed man, who appeared to be the commander, was the first to leap ashore, and addressing us without ceremony, said that his name was David Thompson and that he was one of the partners in the North West Company.

Thompson and his men were warmly welcomed by former Nor'Wester Duncan McDougall, who was in charge of Fort Astoria. However, some of Astor's men were uneasy

On July 3, 1811, after building a cedar canoe, Thompson and his men departed Kettle Falls on the Columbia River on their way to the Pacific Ocean. JOSEPH CROSS

about the hospitality accorded to Thompson. Alexander Ross wrote, "M'Dougall received him like a brother; nothing was too good for Mr. Thompson; he had access everywhere; saw & examined everything, and whatever he asked for he got, as if he had been one of ourselves."

Thompson stayed at the fort for about a week, leaving on July 21 to continue his survey of the Columbia River. By August, he had completed the missing portions and could say that he had surveyed and paddled the whole river, from its source to its mouth, a distance of approximately 2,000 miles.

He wrote, "Thus I have fully completed the survey of this part of North America from sea to sea, and by almost innumerable astronomical observations have determined the positions of the Mountains, Lakes and Rivers, and other remarkable places on the northern part of this Continent, the Maps of all of which have been drawn and laid down in geographical position, being now the work of twenty-seven years."

On November 19, Thompson arrived at the rundown Saleesh House, which he rebuilt. He spent the winter there and on February 12, 1812, accompanied by Finan McDonald and 11 others, left by canoe to trade with the Salish, returning a month later. He went on to Kettle Falls, where he built canoes from March 31 to April 21, before heading back east in a six-canoe brigade loaded with 120 packs of furs, each pack weighing 90 pounds.

Thompson crossed Athabasca Pass on May 8 and, after being joined by Charlotte and the children, arrived at Fort William on July 12. Sometime before arriving, he had made a momentous decision about his career, one he was planning to announce at the annual council meeting.

The Eastern Years: 1812–1857

THOMPSON ARRIVED AT FORT WILLIAM just in time for the 1812 council meeting. Thirty-eight partners were present to hear him declare he was retiring from the fur trade and moving with his family to Montreal. Highly respected, Thompson was given a generous retirement package by the partners. For the next three years, in addition to a full share of the company's profits, he would receive a salary of 100 pounds a year to compile his astronomical observations and produce maps for the NWC. After the three years passed, his official retirement would begin, and for the next seven years, he would receive the usual allotment given to retired partners: one-hundredth of the company's annual profit.

The War of 1812

On July 18, word reached Fort William that the US had declared war on Great Britain a month previously. This greatly concerned the Nor'Westers, who knew that the primary battleground would be Upper Canada (today's Ontario). But what had brought the two countries back to war after only 30 years of peace? Historians suggest that rather than a single dominant issue, there were a number of American grievances leading to the conflict, including the British naval blockade to trade, its "Right to Search" policy toward American vessels, and the American dream to expand northward by conquering Upper Canada.

"We were warned to be on our guard; this made us all look very serious, for the whole returns of the Company were yet here, getting ready to be sent to Montreal," wrote Thompson. Quickly, furs valued at 200,000 pounds were loaded on 47 canoes, as men became "alarmed at the chance of being made prisoners." On August 15, in a canoe brigade guarded by armed Nor'Westers, Thompson headed east along the north shore of Lake Superior, re-surveying it along the way. The brigade hugged the shore between Sault Ste. Marie and the French River, evading the armed American vessels *Tigress* and *Scorpion*, which were patrolling Lake Huron. Once they were out of the war-zone waters of the Great Lakes, Thompson wrote, "We held ourselves to be safe."

Montreal and Terrebonne

Soon after Thompson arrived in Montreal, he took care of two personal priorities. First was the baptism of Charlotte and his children on September 30 at St. Gabriel Street Church, a Scottish Presbyterian church founded in Montreal by leading members of the NWC. A month later, he formally solemnized his marriage to Charlotte in a Christian ceremony at their two-storey brick home in the small village of Terrebonne, located about 30 miles northeast of Montreal.

Ten years earlier, Simon McTavish had purchased the seigneury of Terrebonne, along the Rivière des Mille Îles. Under McTavish, Terrebonne had become an important NWC centre and depot, although McTavish never lived in Terrebonne himself. After McTavish's death in 1804, retired NWC partner Roderick Mackenzie had managed the seigneury for the McTavish estate.

Thompson, arriving when Britain was still at war with the US, joined the local militia and became its ensign major on October 31, 1812. During the next three months, he designed a "cannon frame" to carry nine-pound guns fired from sleighs on snow or ice during winter campaigns. He delivered the plans and a scale model to Sir George Prevost, governor-in-chief of British North America, in January 1813, before starting to design a similar device for larger guns. "It is a most ingenious contrivance," wrote Lieutenant Colonel Ralph Bruyeres, commander of the Royal Engineers in the Canadas, in a letter to Prevost.

Thompson, who had spent most of his life trekking in the isolated northern wilderness, fit easily into the "civilized" world, even as he fondly remembered the past. At a Montreal dinner party given by William McGillivray, Dr. John J. Bigsby observed how Thompson's great storytelling skills could "create a wilderness and people it with warring savages, or climb the Rocky Mountains with you in a snow-storm, so clearly and palpably that only shut your eyes and you can hear the crack of the rifle or feel the snow flakes on your cheeks as he talks."

Bigsby recalled how Thompson enthralled guests with a story about travelling through an ice tunnel. "He told us in the far northwest, near the Arctic circle, the ice forms over a river, and the water sometimes deserts its bed. There is a dry channel, with a high arch of rough ice overhead, tinted white, green and earth-coloured, if the banks are lofty. He said he had travelled for the best part of a mile in such a tunnel, simply because it was the best road."

At the dinner party, when McGillivray had been asked if there were any truths to accounts of "dancing pheasants" in the Northwest, it was Thompson who responded that he had repeatedly stumbled upon a "pheasant's ball" among the glades on the eastern flanks of the Rocky Mountains, adding:

> The pheasants choose a beech for the dance, a tree with boughs, several on [the] same level, and only full leafed at their ends. The feathered spectators group around. Six or seven pheasants

step on the trembling stage and begin to stamp, and prance, and twinkle their little feet like so many Bayadères, skipping with *balancez et chassez* from bough to bough; or they sit with curtsey and flutter, arching their glowing necks, and oping and closing their wings in concert; but, in truth, the dance is indescribable, most singular, and laughable. When it lasted ten minutes, a new set of performers step forward, and the exhibition may last a couple of hours.

Thompson also talked to Bigsby about the famous 1782 murder of Swiss-born fur trader Jean-Étienne Waddens by Peter Pond at Île-à-la-Crosse, referring to Pond's disposition as "violent and rapacious." According to Thompson, Waddens was much liked by Indians and therefore in Pond's way:

He [Waddens] was trading with a small outfit from government and a permit, as was the practice. At a portage called Isle la Crosse, Pond and a confederate agreed to get rid of him. It was affected thus. They invited Wadanne to sup with them alone in their tent. Over their cups the conspirators engaged in a fierce mock quarrel, both seized their guns. Wadanne tried to mediate and was 'accidently' shot in the scuffle. His thigh-bone was broken, and he died a few days after. Mrs. Wadanne was close by; but the mischief was done before she could interfere. I saw her daughter afterwards at Fort La Pluie [Rainy Lake House]. Pond was brought down and lodged in Montreal gaol but was acquitted for want of evidence.

Years later, Bigsby wrote about Thompson: "No living person possesses a tithe of his information, respecting the Hudson Bay countries . . . Never mind his Bunyan-like face and cropped hair, he has a very powerful mind and a singular faculty of picture-taking."

Barely 16 months after arriving in Terrebonne, tragedy struck the Thompson family. Two of their young children died from ringworm, a common parasite. John, who was 5 years old, died on January 11, 1814; Emma, aged 7, died on February 22. In his journal, a devastated Thompson wrote about John, "[I] had a Coffin of Oak made for him . . . a beautiful boy . . . This loss has plunged us in deep affliction especially his poor Mother." Later, he wrote of Emma, "[I] buried my poor little daughter close touching her little Brother John in the same Grave . . . an amiable, innocent little girl, too good for the world . . . God Almighty, the Saviour of the World, bless them both."

The Great "Map of Dreams"

Thompson spent two years (1812–14) working on the grand map he had dreamed about creating for years. Using his astronomical observations and calculations, he laid out the major river systems and mountain ranges from Hudson Bay to Lake Superior to the shores of the Pacific and from the upper Missouri River to the 60th parallel. All 78 of the NWC's trading posts were marked on the map, identified

The Great Hall is one of 46 reconstructed buildings on the 225-acre site of the world's largest fur-trade post at Fort William Historical Park in Thunder Bay, Ontario. ELLE ANDRA-WARNER

with the abbreviation NWCo, as were the direction of the river flows, shown by arrows.

Drawn to a scale of 15 miles to 1 inch, the great map measured 6 feet 9 inches by 10 feet 4 inches and was titled "Map of the North-West Territory of the Province of Canada From actual Survey during the years 1792–1812." The map showed the full grandeur of the NWC's empire. At the 1814 rendezvous, Thompson's huge map was hung in the great hall at Fort William, where it remained for many years.

After the historic merger of the HBC and NWC in 1821, the HBC brought Thompson's map to England and gave it to

Britain's leading cartographic firm, Aaron Arrowsmith. The firm revised their map of North America, but gave no credit to Thompson. Thompson's great "map of dreams" became the foundation for future maps of western Canada and is on display at the Ontario Provincial Archives in Toronto.

Upper Canada: Williamstown

The War of 1812 ended on December 24, 1814, with the Treaty of Ghent. One of the treaty terms was the establishment of an international commission to delineate the boundary between the US and British North America. It required both Britain and the US to be represented by an astronomer-surveyor. Thompson let it be known that he wanted the position.

In October 1815, Thompson moved his family to Upper Canada to settle in Williamstown, a Scottish Loyalist area of Glengarry County. The move had been triggered by the news that he would be appointed astronomer-surveyor for Britain on the boundary commission.

Williamstown was located along the Raisin River, about five miles north of the St. Lawrence. Like Terrebonne, it was populated by many retired Nor'Westers like Hugh "Laird" McGillis and Duncan Cameron. In 1816, John McDonald of Garth, Thompson's brother-in-law, settled there, as did Finan McDonald, Thompson's long-time NWC assistant, in 1827.

In Williamstown, Thompson purchased a house and

100-acre farm from the estate of the Reverend John Bethune (an ancestor of the well-known Dr. Norman Bethune). The reverend, who had previously lived in Terrebonne, had moved to Williamstown in 1787, some say to claim the 3,000-acre land grant given to him for being chaplain in a Loyalist unit during the American Revolution.

When Bethune died in Williamstown on September 1815, his widow Véronique Waddens (daughter of the murdered fur trader Jean-Étienne Waddens and his French-Canadian wife, Marie Josephe De Guire) sold the estate to the Thompsons. Today, the home is known as the Bethune-Thompson House, a National Historic Site owned by Ontario Heritage Trust.

The International Boundary Commission

Thompson was 46 years old when he began his work as chief astronomer and surveyor for the International Boundary Commission in mid-January 1817. For the next 10 years, he would be absent from Williamstown and his family for most of each year. The roots of the International Boundary Commission stretched back to the American War of Independence and the 1783 Treaty of Paris that ended the war. However, it wasn't until the Treaty of Ghent that a joint American-British survey commission was established to resolve the boundary issues. The commission's task was to organize teams from both Britain and the US to survey the proposed border between the colonies of British North America and the US.

Thompson was part of the British team tasked with completing the survey under Articles 6 and 7 of the treaty. The Article 6 work was carried out between 1817 and 1821, beginning near St. Regis on the St. Lawrence and ending at Sault Ste. Marie, Ontario. Fieldwork on the surveys under Article 7 began in 1822, going west from Sault Ste. Marie and ending in 1825 on Lake of the Woods. The survey work was followed by many months spent writing reports. Thompson, who was the only person to work the full tenure of the commission, continued preparing maps and reports until 1827.

Thompson's role included technical surveying duties as well as much of the planning and logistics required for the team to work in the Canadian wilderness. David J. Cooper, from the US National Park Service at Grand Portage, writes:

> To his men, Thompson's experience and steady leadership were a great comfort ... A font of wilderness knowledge, from native customs and languages to the hazards of the voyage, Thompson played many roles during the survey. For example, he designed and helped build the survey party's boat; cultivated native allies by giving them gifts and negotiating for their services; provided for the care of a sick boatman; read the Bible in an 'extraordinary' French to his voyageurs; shot a swimming bear from the bow of his canoe; reminisced about a former narrow escape from death while bison hunting; and showed great manners and courtesy to native occupants of the region.

The commission's work was deadly at times. During September 1819, while surveying in the marshes along Lake St. Clair, three British members died, and the entire commission, including Thompson, became very ill with chills and high fever, likely with malaria. The dead included Thompson's assistant, a British boatman and 50-year-old British commissioner John Ogilvy, who became sick on September 12 and died 10 days later in Amherstburg.

In mid-September, Thompson wrote in his journal, "Found myself so ill that twice fainted away in attempting to stand up." For 21 days, he was extremely weak and delirious with a high fever. When he was able, he returned to Williamstown, where he remained "feeble and out of health" all winter. In light of the tragedy, when the commission resumed work the following year, it added a medical doctor to the team, 28-year-old Dr. John J. Bigsby from England, who was also a geologist.

In 1822, the commission began the survey for Article 7, delineating the border from Sault Ste. Marie through to Lake of the Woods by the Manitoba border. At this time, Thompson was appointed the only official astronomer for the entire commission.

Thompson used his years of wilderness mapmaking experience to tailor his survey methods to the terrain. While travelling by water, he calculated the distance using a patent log, a propeller-like measuring device towed behind a boat. However, west of Grand Portage, according to Bigsby, his calculations were "based on the average speed of the north canoes with six paddlers at 110 metres (120 yards) per minute. Bigsby wrote that Thompson attained his measurements by fixing "principal points on the lake at about equal distances from each other, by observation for latitude and longitude, and then by filling up the intervals by compass and log or estimate."

Disputed boundary areas under Article 7 included the Lake Superior to Lake of the Woods section, which was not resolved until the Treaty of 1842. What was not in dispute was the valuable service that Thompson had given to both Britain and the US. David Adams, the American surveyor on the commission, called him, "A gentleman, whom for his rectitude of heart, honesty of disposition, integrity of character and abilities in his profession, I shall ever hold in the highest estimation."

Thompson the Entrepreneur

After the commission work geared down, Thompson turned his energies to opportunities in Williamstown. During his years in the West, Thompson had thrived on the challenges of working in the wilderness. His sense of adventure and desire to break new ground were now directed toward business ventures. A wealthy man, Thompson invested in land, sold lots to Glengarry residents and then held their mortgages. And he continued to look for opportunities to increase his income and provide work for his children.

Besides being a land developer, Thompson operated a sheep, pig and cattle farm, set up two potash companies, took on supply contracts, operated two general stores and became Justice of the Peace for Glengarry County.

However, things started to go badly for Thompson in 1829, starting with a contract he had made with the British to supply the commissariat depot in Montreal with firewood. Everything seemed to go wrong: labour problems plagued the project, some cordwood was cut too short to sell, and rafts carrying the cordwood ran aground, broke up, anchored elsewhere or went missing. Thompson spent September and October trying to find wood to fulfill the contract. In mid-September, he wrote, "This is a sad business and I pray God in his mercy that no more may happen." The job was finished November 4, months behind schedule and with Thompson taking a loss on the venture.

Within three years, Thompson's financial condition had worsened because of a "perfect storm" of economic events. The NWC had gone bankrupt, resulting in the loss of his life savings. A worldwide recession and then depression hit Upper and Lower Canada. Businesses failed, and people stopped paying their debts. Thompson had given credit to 148 people, including 60 loans to buy farms, but now most were defaulting on these loans. Thompson was in a precarious financial position. With substantially reduced income, how could he make the mortgage payments on his lands, now worth less than the purchase price?

To pay his bills, support his family and keep his businesses operating, Thompson returned to work as a surveyor. Between 1833 and 1836, he landed a number of surveying contracts, hiring his son Henry as his assistant. He surveyed Lake St. Francis, the provincial boundary from the St. Lawrence to the Ottawa River, and did exploratory line surveys of the Eastern Townships of Lower Canada for the British American Land Company.

Despite his efforts, Thompson was unable to pay off his debts, and by the end of 1835, his world was collapsing. In 1836, the court seized all his lands, businesses and the family home of 20 years and sold them on September 29.

Before the sale, Thompson and Charlotte had moved with 7 of their 10 children to Montreal. Thompson continued working as a surveyor, producing a series of maps of the St. Lawrence and Great Lakes, making detailed maps of waterways between Upper Canada and the US and surveying the Muskoka district to find a feasible canal route between Georgian Bay and the Ottawa River. During the summers of 1838 to 1842, Thompson worked on contracts for the governments of Upper and Lower Canada (after 1840, Canada West and Canada East), surveying Lake St. Peter, Lake of Two Mountains and Lac Saint-Louis, plus portions of the Ottawa River.

After 1842, Thompson's financial problems returned. On January 28, 1843, he wrote in his journal, "We are without wood." On April 29, his journal reads, "I am the morrow

73 years old and so destitute that I have not where to buy a loaf of Bread." By fall, he was selling his possessions to support the family.

Thompson lobbied unsuccessfully to get a small government pension, a publisher for his maps or work at other positions. In 1843, the British government paid him 150 pounds for a new version of his maps; however, they ignored his advice on the Oregon boundaries. (In 1846, Britain ceded most of the Oregon territory, including the Columbia Basin, to the US.)

The Final Years

In October 1845, at the age of 75 years, Thompson began writing a narrative based on his wilderness journals from his time in the West. Still an entrepreneur, Thompson began looking for subscribers to underwrite the publishing costs. His prospectus in the *Montreal Gazette* on October 16, 1846, read:

> To be published as soon as a sufficient number of Subscribers are obtained to justify the undertaking, THE TRAVELS OF DAVID THOMPSON, during the Twenty-eight consecutive Years in the Northern parts of this Continent; of which twenty-five years were employed in the Exploration and Survey of Countries not then known, or the Survey and Examination of Countries known to the Fur Traders, and six years at several Trading Posts. The last six years of his travels were in different parts of the Rocky Mountains, the discovery of the noble

source of the Columbia River and its course to the Pacific Ocean, and also its great branches. Settlements of the North West Company were made by him four years before any person from the US settled on the Columbia River . . .

This will not be in a dry detail. Many curious facts will, for the first time, be given to the public, which will interest the reader. The extent of the Forests and of the great Plains, with the Animals, Birds, Fishes, &c., peculiar to each sections, will be noticed. And also the various Tribes of Indians which inhabit these Countries, their several Languages, their Religious Opinions, Manners and Mode of Life, the place and extent of their Hunting Grounds, and the changes which have taken place by the fortune of War, or other causes, will be given.

The above countries underwent a personal Survey, with good instruments, and the position of numerous places were determined by astronomical observations, the Journals of which are complete . . . and thus form a curious and extensive collection of all that can fall under the observations of a Traveller.

The book promised to deliver an incredible journey into the mysterious North, but sadly, by March 1847, not one person had subscribed, and Thompson pulled the prospectus. He refused, however, to be denied the opportunity to leave a written legacy of his wilderness years, and continued with the mammoth project.

Sometime before August 1846, Thompson and Charlotte moved in with their daughter Elizabeth and her husband, William Scott. In 1849, the Thompsons resided for a time with their son Joshua and his wife, before returning back

A life-sized bronze statue of David Thompson
and Charlotte Small Thompson at Invermere,
BC, pays tribute to their long-lasting marriage.
ROSS MACDONALD

to the Scotts. On April 27, 1850, the Thompsons and their
daughter Eliza moved with the Scotts to Longueuil; days
later, Thompson turned 80 years old.

By 1851, Thompson had lost most of his sight (he had

lost it three years earlier but regained it temporarily) and could hardly read. His incomplete manuscript of 670 pages was still without a publisher. In late February, he made one final journal entry and never wrote again.

Four years later, at age 85, Thompson buried another of his children when his 42-year-old son Henry died on October 23, 1855.

When the Scotts moved to Elkhart, Indiana, after William accepted a position as engineer on a canal project, Thompson and Charlotte stayed in Longueuil with Eliza and her husband, Dalhousie Landel, the cargo master of the Grand Trunk Railway. Although he lacked worldly possessions, Thompson spent his last years with his beloved Charlotte, living in the comfortable surroundings of the Landel home.

On February 10, 1857, Thompson died at home at 87 years of age. Charlotte died three months later, on May 4. They are buried side by side in Montreal's Mount Royal Cemetery in the Landel family plot. David and Charlotte Thompson had been married for 58 years and, according to historians, had the longest pre-Confederation marriage on record.

It would be 1916 before David Thompson's *Narrative* was published by the Champlain Society. The book is one of North America's finest examples of early travel writing—a legacy to a fascinating historical era and to the legendary man who recorded it.

Epilogue

NO PAINTINGS OR IMAGES ARE KNOWN to exist of David Thompson. Descriptions of his appearance come from contemporaries like Dr. John J. Bigsby. After their first meeting in Montreal, Bigsby described Thompson as "plainly dressed, quiet, and observant. His figure was short and compact, and his black hair worn long all round, and cut square, as if by one stroke of the shears, just above the eyebrows. His complexion was of the gardener's ruddy brown while the expression of his deeply furrowed features was friendly and intelligent, but his cut-short nose gave him an odd look." A few years later, Bigsby compared Thompson's weathered face and now iron-grey locks to "Moses in the wilderness of Sinai."

Thompson's genuine voice, however, comes through in the vivid writing of his epic *Narrative* and in accounts of his storytelling. After Thompson's death, his son Joshua sold the handwritten *Narrative* manuscript to Charles Lindsey, the editor of the *Toronto Leader*. It remained in his desk drawer until a young geologist named Joseph Burr Tyrrell became curious about the mapmaker who was listed on the government maps. Tyrrell purchased the manuscript for $400 in 1888.

Although he never received recognition for his landmark work during his lifetime, Thompson is now honoured in many ways throughout North America in geographical landmarks, monuments, statues, cairns, plaques, museum exhibitions, paintings, songs and a Canadian postage stamp.

In recent years, an initiative known as the North American David Thompson Bicentennial Partnership—with partners in Canada, the US and Great Britain—was formed to increase understanding of the significance of Thompson, commemorate his life and accomplishments and, during the years 2007 to 2011, promote bicentennial events honouring his accomplishments from 1807 to 1811. Events in North America have included canoe brigades, beginning with the 2007 Columbia Brigade that paddled from Canal Flats to Trail, BC. The 2008 David Thompson Brigade retraced the lengthy route from Rocky Mountain House to Fort William (present-day Thunder Bay) using traditional 25-foot north canoes, or *canots du nord*, the

Epilogue

Retracing the route from Rocky Mountain House to Fort William, the 300 participants in the 2008 David Thompson Brigade covered 3,300 kilometres and crossed 4 provinces in 63 days.
FORT WILLIAM HISTORICAL PARK

small, lightweight canoes used by the NWC on inland waterways west of Lake Superior. Plans are under way for the 2010 David Thompson Brigade, from Fort William to Montreal, and the 2011 David Thompson Columbia Brigade, which will paddle the Columbia River from Invermere, BC (the site of Thompson's Kootenae House) to Astoria, Oregon, arriving by July 15, 2011, the 200th anniversary of Thompson's arrival at the mouth of the Columbia.

The story of Thompson would not be complete without acknowledging his remarkable wife, Charlotte. According to cartographer Andy Korsos, who has mapped the extensive travels of Thompson and Charlotte, it is likely she travelled

135

in excess of 42,000 kilometres (27,000 miles) by canoe, foot and horseback.

In 1927, on the 70th anniversary of Thompson's death, the government of Canada formally recognized his achievements when the Historic Sites and Monuments Board designated him a person of historic importance. The inscription on a plaque in Jasper National Park reads:

> Born in London, Thompson served both the Hudson's Bay Company (1784–1797) and the North West Company (1797–1815) as trader, explorer and surveyor. One of the world's greatest geographers he accurately mapped the main travel routes through some 1,700,000 square miles of Canadian and American West, in the process journeying some 50,000 miles by canoe, by horse and foot. His great map of the West and his Narrative, edited by J. B. Tyrrell for the Champlain Society (1916), are lasting monuments to his genius. He died at Longueuil.

Thompson's legacy has crossed the Atlantic Ocean back to his ancestral home in Wales. He is featured in an hour-long episode in the 2009 BBC documentary series *Roy Mears' Northern Wilderness*, which tells the stories of Britons who "charted the wilderness of North America." Mears, a world-renowned bushcraft and survival expert, retraced Thompson's footsteps and says of him, "Without the benefit of Google Maps, he was able to grasp the scale of the continent . . . I think the people of Wales should be very proud of him. Wales can claim him as a hero."

Bibliography

Books and Articles

Andra-Warner, Elle. *Hudson's Bay Company Adventures: Tales of Canada's Fur Traders*. Victoria: Heritage House, 2009.

Barnard, Stuart. "Insightful Exploration: An Early Explorer's Perspective on Western Aboriginals." *Lethbridge Undergraduate Research Journal* 2, no. 1 (2007), http://lurj.org/vol2n1.php.

Bigsby, John J. *The Shoe and Canoe: Pictures of Travel in the Canadas*. London: Chapman and Hall, 1850.

Bowen, Stephen R. "In the Footsteps of David Thompson." *The Beaver*, June/July 2002, 13–19.

Burpee, Lawrence J. "Grand Portage." *Minnesota History Magazine* 12, no. 4 (1931): 359–72.

Campbell, Marjorie Wilkins. *The North West Company*. Toronto: Douglas & McIntyre, 1957. Reprinted 1983.

Cooper, David J. "Of Sextants and Satellites: David Thompson and the Grand Portage GIS Study." Paper presented at CRLS Colloquium 2004, Kenora, Ontario.

Franchère, Gabriel. *Narrative of a Voyage to the Northwest Coast of America, in the years 1811, 1812, 1813, and 1814*. New York: Redfield, 1854. Reprint, Chicago: The Lakeside Press, 1954.

Hearne, Samuel. *A Journey from Prince of Wales's Fort in Hudson Bay to the Northern Ocean*. London: A. Strahan and T. Cadell, 1795; Toronto: Champlain Society, 1911.

Houston, C.S. "The First Smallpox Epidemic on the Canadian Plains: In the fur-traders' words." *The Canadian Journal of Infectious*

Diseases and Medical Microbiology 11, no. 2 (March/April 2000): 112–15.

Huck, Barbara, et al. *Exploring the Fur Trade Routes of North America: Discover the Highways that Opened a Continent.* Winnipeg: Heartland Associates, 2002.

Innis, Harold Adams. *The Fur Trade in Canada: An Introduction to Canadian Economic History.* New Haven: Yale University Press, 1930; Toronto, University of Toronto Press, 1977.

Irving, Washington. *Astoria: Adventures in the Pacific Northwest.* London: KPI, 1839. Reprint, Norman: University of Nebraska Press, 1964.

Jenish, D'Arcy. *Epic Wanderer: David Thompson and the Mapping of the Canadian West.* Scarborough: Doubleday Canada, 2003.

Lass, William E. "How the Forty Ninth-Parallel became the International Boundary." *Minnesota History Magazine* 44, no. 6 (1975): 209-219.

MacKay, Douglas. *The Honourable Company.* Toronto: McClelland and Stewart, 1966.

MacLaren, Ian. "David Thompson's Imaginative Mapping of the Canadian Northwest 1784–1812." *Ariel* 15 (1984): 89-106.

Malainey, Mary E. "The Gros Ventre/Fall Indians in Historical and Archaeological Interpretation." *The Canadian Journal of Native Studies* XXV, 1 (2005): 155–83.

Marwick, Ernest W. "William Tomison, Pioneer of the Fur Trade." *Alberta Historical Review* 10, no. 4 (1962): 1–8.

Morrison, Jean, ed. *Lake Superior to Rainy Lake: Three Centuries of Fur Trade History.* Thunder Bay: Thunder Bay Historical Museum Society, 2003.

———. *Superior Rendezvous-Place: Fort William in the Canadian Fur Trade.* Toronto: Natural Heritage Books, 2001.

Bibliography

Morton, W.L. "The North West Company Pedlars Extraordinary." *Minnesota History Magazine* 40, no. 4 (1966): 157–65.

Nisbet, Jack. *Sources of the River: Tracking David Thompson across Western North America*. Seattle: Sasquatch, 1994.

Nute, Grace Lee. *Rainy River Country*. St. Paul: Minnesota Historical Society Press, 1950.

———. *The Voyageur's Highway*. St. Paul: Minnesota Historical Society Press, 1941.

Pollitt, Frances L. "Mapping the International Boundary between British Canadas and the United States: the letters and maps of David Thompson 1817–1827." Paper presented at World Library and Information Congress: 74th IFLA General Conference and Council, August 10–14, 2008, Québec, Canada.

Ray, Arthur J. *I Have Lived Here Since the World Began: An Illustrated History of Canada's Native People*. Toronto: Lester Publishing & Key Porter Books, 1996.

Thompson, David. *Columbia Journals*. Edited by Barbara Belyea. Montreal and Kingston: McGill-Queen's University Press, 2007.

———. *David Thompson's Narrative of His Explorations in Western America, 1784–1812*. Edited by J.B. Tyrrell. Toronto: Champlain Society, 1916.

———. *David Thompson's Narrative, 1784–1812*. Edited by Richard Glover. Toronto: Champlain Society, 1962.

———. *The Writings of David Thompson, Volume 1: The Travels, 1850 Version*. Edited by William E. Moreau. Montreal and Kingston: McGill-Queen's University Press, 2009.

Tyrell, Joseph B. *A Brief Narrative of the Journeys of David Thompson in North-Western America*. Toronto: Copp Clark Company, 1888.

Van Kirk, Sylvia. *Many Tender Ties: Women in Fur-Trade Society in Western Canada, 1670–1870*. Winnipeg: Watson & Dwyer, 1980.

Wonders, William. "Orkney and the "Nor-Waast." *Alberta History Review* 41, no. 1 (1993): 3–13.

Selected Websites

David Thompson Things. http://www.davidthompsonthings.com

Hudson's Bay Company Archives. http://www.gov.mb.ca.chc/archives.hbca.

North American David Thompson Bicentennials. http://www.davidthompson200.org.

North West Journal. http://www.northwestjournal.ca.

Orkneyjar: The Heritage of the Orkney Islands. http://www.orkneyjar.com.

Parks Canada. David Thompson: Discover Canada's Greatest Explorer. http://www.pc.gc.ca/culture/proj.dt/index_e.asp.

Index

Acknowledgements

As I write this, I am sitting by the Bow River in Calgary, perhaps near the spot where David Thompson camped with the Peigan over 200 years ago. Even though he died over 150 years ago, Thompson—who linked a continent with his mapmaking—today links a diverse group of people who recognize and celebrate his accomplishments. I am honoured to have connected with a number of them in creating this book.

In particular, my deepest appreciation to the historians, authors, researchers, writers and cartographers who have told Thompson's story and provided valuable resources for others to access. I'd also like to acknowledge research and online resources, including the Champlain Society, Hudson's Bay Company Archives, federal and provincial archives, museums and historical associations, Parks Canada, the North American David Thompson Bicentennial Partnership and the US National Park Service.

Warm thanks go to Ross MacDonald, David Malaher, Rodney Brown, Don McMaster, Ron Peniuk, James Cross and Andy Korsos. Special thanks are also due to Marty Mascarin and Fort William Historical Park in Thunder Bay for generous assistance in providing access to Fort William, the world's largest reconstructed fur-trading post, and its resources.

Thank you to Rodger Touchie and Vivian Sinclair at Heritage House Publishing for providing me with the opportunity to write this book, and deepest appreciation to my editor, Lesley Reynolds, for her excellent editing skills in enhancing and bringing clarity to the manuscript—she was wonderful to work with.

Special recognition goes to my children for their encouragement and to my husband, Glenn, for his ongoing support (including making gourmet meals and bringing coffee and goodies) while I was immersed in this project.

About the Author

Elle Andra-Warner is an author, journalist and photographer based in Thunder Bay, Ontario. She writes about history, culture, travel, people and business and is the bestselling author of books about Canadian history, including *Hudson's Bay Company Adventures* and *The Mounties*, also published by Heritage House. Her award-winning articles appear in major publications, and her newspaper columns on business, travel and history have been in print since 1994.

A political studies graduate, Elle is a member of the Professional Writers Association of Canada, Travel Media of Canada, the Writers Union of Canada and the Canadian Freelance Union and is on the board of directors of the Thunder Bay Historical Museum Society. She has given journalism workshops throughout Canada, been an online guest journalism lecturer for UCLA and co-edits the Thunder Bay Historical Museum Society's journal, *Papers & Records*.

Estonian by heritage, Elle was born in a post–Second World War United Nations displaced persons camp in Eckernforde, West Germany. She came to Canada with her parents, settling in Port Arthur, Ontario (now Thunder Bay). Elle is married and the mother of three daughters—Tania, Tami and Cindi. She has one grandson, Alexander.